Diving & Snorkeling

Cozumel

George S. Lewbel

Larry R. Martin

LONELY PLANET PUBLICATIONS
Melbourne • Oakland • London • Paris

Diving & Snorkeling Cozumel
- A Lonely Planet Pisces Book

3rd Edition – July 1998
2nd Edition – 1991, Gulf Publishing Company
1st Edition – 1984 PBC International, Inc.

Published by
Lonely Planet Publications
192 Burwood Road, Hawthorn, Victoria 3122, Australia

Other offices
150 Linden Street, Oakland, California 94607, USA
10A Spring Place, London NW5 3BH, UK
71 bis rue du Cardinal Lemoine, 75005 Paris, France

Photographs by
Larry R. Martin, George S. Lewbel and Steve Rosenberg

Front cover photograph
Tormentos Reef, Larry R. Martin

ISBN 0 86442 574 0

text © George S. Lewbel, Larry R. Martin,
    and Lonely Planet 1998
maps © Lonely Planet 1998
photographs © photographers as indicated 1998

Printed by H&Y Printing Ltd., Hong Kong

Contents

Introduction **9**

Cozumel Practicalities **11**

History **11**
Natural History **14**
Weather **14**
Cozumel Island Today **15**
Hotels **16**
Transportation **18**
Foreign Exchange, Language, Dining & Shopping **19**
Documents **22**

Diving in Cozumel **23**

Typical Dive Operations **23**
Useful Dive Techniques **27**
Cozumel Diving Recommendations **30**
Pisces Rating System for Dives & Divers **31**
Cozumel Dive Sites **32**
  1 Paraíso Reef North **34**
  2 The Junkyard (formerly Airplane Flats) **36**
  3 Paraíso Reef South **38**
  4 Chankanab **40**
  5 Beachcomber Cavern **41**
  6 Tormentos Reef **44**
  7 Yocab Reef **46**
  8 El Paso del Cedral Reef **48**
  9 Tunich **49**
  10 Cardona Reef **51**
  11 San Francisco Reef **53**
  12 Santa Rose Reef **54**
  13 Palancar Reef **55**
  14 Punta Sur **56**
  15 Colombia Reef **58**

16 Maracaibo Reef **59**
17 Colombia Shallows **60**
18 Sand Diver's Secret **62**

Marine Life **66**

Corals **67**
Anemones & Sponges **69**
Fishes **70**
Common Hazardous Marine Animals **71**

Diving Safety **76**

Diving Accidents **76**

Diving Conservation & Awareness **80**

Spearfishing & Hunting Underwater **84**

Dive Services **85**

Index **87**

Authors

George S. Lewbel

George is a retired diving instructor and semi-retired oceanographer who has a day job documenting high-tech products in Silicon Valley. He has been a NOAA aquanaut in saturation dives in the Bahamas; an ice diver off the North Slope of Alaska; an offshore oil-rig fauna specialist in the Gulf of Mexico; a freeloading travel writer in the western Pacific; and a hungry graduate student on the beaches overlooking the submarine canyons of California. As a marine scientist, he has published a variety of papers and technical reports, and as a diver, has sold magazine articles and written guidebooks for several Caribbean islands, including Pisces' *Diving & Snorkeling Guide to Curaçao*. He lives in the Santa Cruz mountains south of San Francisco.

Larry R. Martin

Larry is a senior marine biologist and diving safety officer for LGL Ecological Research Associates of Bryan, Texas. He has conducted research utilizing diving techniques in the Gulf of Mexico, the Caribbean, the Bering Sea, the Alaskan and Canadian Arctic and Antarctica. His work has required diving under Arctic ice, mixed gas diving, and saturation diving. He is a Master scuba instructor and teaches college scuba courses. He lives in Galveston, Texas.

From the Authors

We thank Bill Horn and Donna Mena (Aqua Safari, Cozumel); Ruth Herrera Hernandez (Cozumel Diamond Resort), and Michele Harrison and Pat Noel (Poseidon Ventures Tours, Houston), and Nacho Cureno, manager of the recompression chamber, for their assistance with the third edition of this book. We are especially grateful to the following friends and fellow divers who assisted in the preparation of the second edition: Bill Horn and Ruth Herrera Hernandez; Michele Harrison and Pat Noel; and Carolyn Martin. We wish to say "Gracias!" to the following friends for assistance and encouragement in the production of the first edition of the guide: Pancho Morales (La Ceiba Hotel, Cozumel); Michele Harrison; Dick Tompkins (Aqua Safari); Carlos Sierra (Dive Cozumel, Cozumel); Hal Martin (Scuba World, Houston); Karen Young (Underwater Safaris, Houston); Kit Teague; and Sally Sutherland, Kelly Hildreth, and Pancho Contreras.

From the Publisher

The first two editions of this book were published by PBC International and Gulf Publishing Company. This edition was produced in Lonely Planet's U.S. office as the first Lonely Planet Pisces book. The editor was Roslyn Bullas, assisted by Debra Miller. Hugh D'Andrade created the series design and handled most of the layout, with Scott Summers pitching in. Hugh also designed the cover, and Alex Guilbert created the maps.

Lonely Planet Pisces Books

Lonely Planet acquired the Pisces line of diving and snorkeling books in 1997. The series will be developed and substantially revamped over the next few years, and new titles added. We invite your comments and suggestions.

Warning & Request

Even with dive guides, things change—dive site conditions, regulations, topside information. Nothing stays the same for long. Your feedback on this book will be used to help update future editions and help make the next edition more useful. Excerpts from your correspondence may appear in our newsletter, *Planet Talk*, or in the Postcards section of our website, so please let us know if you don't want your letter published or your name acknowledged.

Correspondence can be addressed to:
Lonely Planet Publications
Pisces Books
150 Linden Street
Oakland, CA 94607

e-mail: info@lonelyplanet.com

L. MARTIN

Introduction

This guide will acquaint you with a variety of dive sites and provide information you can use to decide whether a particular location is appropriate for your abilities and intended dive plan. Hard-core divers who travel fully suited-up with

L. MARTIN

fins, masks, snorkels, and BCs and expect to leap directly from the plane into the water will find this information detailed on a dive-by-dive basis in "Diving in Cozumel." Novice divers and snorkelers will also find a good selection of shallower sites in more protected water.

Read the entire "Diving in Cozumel" section before diving, no matter which sites you're visiting, since some material common to several sites is not repeated for each one. "Diving in Cozumel" and "Diving Safety" should be read thoroughly since they cover both routine and emergency procedures. Photographers and budding marine biologists will want to refer to "Marine Life," which discusses some of the most common and interesting

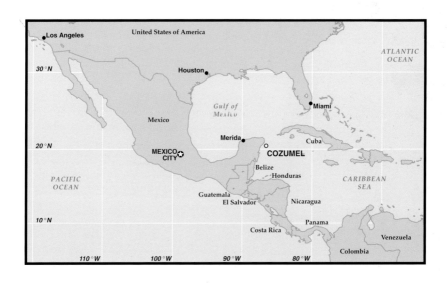

creatures likely to be seen in Cozumel and summarizes current regulations pertaining to divers.

Sooner or later, even the most fanatical divers have to come out of the water. In some places, depending on the shore-based facilities, this can be cause to rejoice or weep. Perhaps you have been to other locations that offered fine diving but could have improved if you'd scraped off everything above the waterline and started over. This most assuredly is not true for Cozumel. Although the diving in Cozumel is spectacular, taking the time to let your gear dry will give you an opportunity to enjoy one of the most charming islands in the Caribbean. "Cozumel Practicalities" offers a brief description of the island's history, geography, scenery, natural history, and some general information on accommodations, services other than diving, shopping, and other useful tips.

Cozumel Practicalities

L. MARTIN

History

Cozumel Island is located near the eastern tip of the Yucatán Peninsula in the Mexican state of Quintana Roo. The island is about 30 miles (40 kilometers) long and about 10 miles (16 kilometers) wide. Due to its proximity to the mainland, the center of Mayan culture, the island was under Mayan influence for many centuries. Even today many residents of Cozumel show a striking resemblance to carved and painted images of Pre-Columbian Mayans, and many locals still speak a Mayan dialect as well as Spanish. The Mayan ruins of El Castillo Real and San Gervasio are found in the jungles on the island, although the most famous and spectacular archaeological sites are on the mainland (Chichén Itzá, Cobá, and Tulum). These sites can be visited on one-day tours leaving from Cozumel; reservations for tours can be made at almost any hotel or at the airport.

The ruins of San Gervasio near the center of the island provide an attraction on those rare days when the sea is too rough or when divers just want some surface time.

The island has long been a favored spot for travelers. In pre-Conquest times it was a religious center for Mayans, and was subsequently visited by such notables as Hernán Cortés (who conquered Mexico for Spain during the 16th century) and a number of pirates who took advantage of the abundant fresh water on the island and the calm, deep waters near the western shore to anchor and rest between raids.

In 1841, John Stephens, a New York lawyer and amateur archaeologist, explored the Yucatán mainland and Cozumel on a quest for clues about the origins of ancient Mayan cities. He and John Catherwood, an illustrator and surveyor, dragged Daguerrotype apparatus around in the blazing sun, chopping vegetation away from the ruins so they could be drawn, photographed and explored. (His account, *Incidents of Travel in Yucatán*, is still in print.) He wrote this about Cozumel:

> Amid all the devastations that attended the progress of the Spaniards in America, none is more complete than that which has swept over the island of Cozumel. When I resolved to visit it I was not aware that it was uninhabited...The whole island was overgrown with trees, and except along the shore or within the clearing around the hut, it was impossible to move in any direction without cutting a path...we came upon what might well be called an iron-bound coast, being a table of rock rising but a few feet above the level of the sea, washed by every storm, until it had become porous and full of holes, and the edges stuck up like points of rusted iron.

More recently, the island has been invaded by thousands of divers seeking clear, warm water. Today Cozumel has a most unusual blend of cultures, successfully integrating divers with the resort industry of modern Mexico and the local Mayan heritage.

L. MARTIN

The typical two-dive boat trip includes a lunch break at one of the popular beaches, thus extending the surface interval between dives.

French grunts, bluestriped grunts, and schoolmaster snappers are often found
together resting out of the current.

Natural History

Both Cozumel and the peninsula are low-lying terraces of limestone covered with jungle. The limestone is derived largely from coral that has been solidified and compressed into hard rock over the eons. You can see the fossilized imprints of shells and corals from ancient reefs that make up the limestone if you look carefully along the shore. Much of the coast of Cozumel (especially along the western side) has no sandy beaches but is made up of eroded limestone or **ironshore** (the "iron-bound coast" Stephens referred to). On the eastern side, sandy beaches cover the ironshore in many areas. The limestone is porous, retaining rainwater like a sponge and slowly dissolving. As a result, a halo of fresh water is sometimes seen in the ocean near some spots on the coast. The jungle is dotted with fresh-water springs, caverns, wells, and pools (*cenotes*), which may contain brackish or fresh water depending on the level of the water table and the amount of sea-water intruding through passageways in the rock. At the southern tip of the island, salt marshes create a swampy environment that attracts and holds tourists' vehicles like a magnet.

The island is separated from the mainland by a channel only 12 miles (19 kilometers) wide. On most nights, if you look to the west, you can see the lights of the Yucatán coast from the shores of Cozumel. Most of the mainland coast is still solid jungle (yes, the real kind with hanging vines, poisonous snakes, and parrots and monkeys in the treetops); the only clearings are an occasional ranch or farm and the *cenotes*. If you go hiking, look out for snakes and don't sit on fire ant hills. Fire ants are small, ordinary-looking insects that are to other ants as chili peppers are to tomatoes.

Weather

Due to the rather constant temperature of the water currents that sweep around the island, the climate on Cozumel is predictable although not entirely stable. The average annual air temperature is about 80°F (27°C), and you can expect temperatures in the high 80s to low 90s°F (about 32°C) in July and August, and in the mid-70s°F (about 24°C) in December and January. Water temperatures range from about 77-82°F (25-28°C). However, December and January can see cold fronts from the Continent that can create windy, cloudy and cold weather. A cooling breeze usually blows day and night. Afternoon thundershowers are common but seldom last more than an hour. Fall sometimes brings hurricanes to the Caribbean, but their paths usually bypass Cozumel to the east.

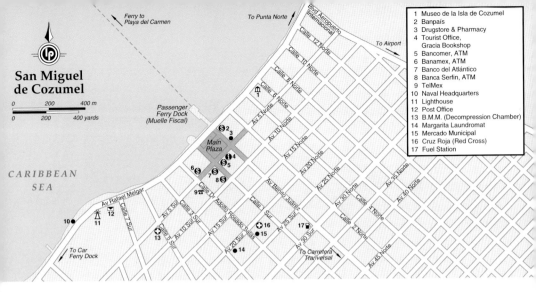

Ferry to
Playa del Carmen

To Punta Norte

To Airport

1 Museo de la Isla de Cozumel
2 Banpaís
3 Drugstore & Pharmacy
4 Tourist Office,
   Gracia Bookshop
5 Bancomer, ATM
6 Banamex, ATM
7 Banco del Atlántico
8 Banca Serfin, ATM
9 TelMex
10 Naval Headquarters
11 Lighthouse
12 Post Office
13 B.M.M. (Decompression Chamber)
14 Margarita Laundromat
15 Mercado Municipal
16 Cruz Roja (Red Cross)
17 Fuel Station

San Miguel de Cozumel

0   200   400 m
0   200   400 yards

Passenger
Ferry Dock
(Muelle Fiscal)

Main
Plaza

CARIBBEAN
SEA

To Car
Ferry Dock

To Carretera
Transversal

Cozumel Island Today

About half of the western-facing shore of Cozumel has been developed into a dense strip of modern hotels along a single road that runs within a few hundred feet of the beach. The strip is separated from the jungle by the road. Taxis patrol this strip day and night, dueling with brave tourists on mopeds.

The hotel row runs north and south from San Miguel de Cozumel, the only town on the island. New resorts have also sprung up near the southern tip of Cozumel, much closer to the prime reefs (Palancar, Colombia, Santa Rosa) than the hotels in town. San Miguel is a typical small Mexican town in some respects, with tiny shops, narrow streets, and a pretty central plaza. In the last few years, however, San Miguel has had to come to grips with its international position as the main service center for an island besieged with divers year round. By and large, it has made the adjustment gracefully. There are many small, inexpensive hotels in town within walking distance of the plaza, restaurants ranging from very inexpensive to fairly expensive, several department stores and markets, liquor stores, a number of dive shops (look for the red and white divers' flag everywhere), car and moped rental agencies, and the ever-present Mexican curio and handicraft shops.

The larger hotels outside town have their own shops and restaurants, and it's possible to spend your entire vacation without venturing into town if you stay in one of the beachfront resorts. You'll be missing a good bet, though, if you don't go into town at least one evening to shop and look around.

L. MARTIN

The hotel row south of town is popular with divers because of the convenient dive sites just off the beach.

Hotels

Virtually all of the hotels on the island cater to divers. They can be divided fairly easily into two general categories: luxury (resort) hotels and simpler, less expensive hotels. Condominiums are also available, and tend toward luxury.

The luxury hotels are located along the waterfront to the north and south of town. They generally have every amenity that one would expect in an international facility, including swimming pools, air-conditioned rooms, restaurants and gift shops. Many of the luxury hotels have dive shops on the premises, and most of them have easy entries and exits (such as concrete steps) at the waterline so you can go diving right in front of the hotel.

The simpler hotels are located within several blocks of the plaza. Some are air-conditioned, some have restaurants (but are within easy walking distance of dozens of other restaurants), and all are much less expensive than the luxury hotels. The simpler hotels usually do not have dive shops on the premises, but nearly all have some working arrangement with one or more dive shop, so you can arrange equipment rental and boat diving through them. Most of the simpler hotels are located near the center of town, within walking distance of dive shops.

Because all the reefs mentioned in this book are south of town, and because nearly all dive operators run boats to the south every day, hotels to the north of town are decidedly less desirable for divers. The boat rides are longer the farther north you go, and many operators will not pick you up north of town. That means worrying about missing the boat in the morning, and salty, wet taxi rides at the end of the day.

A few problems seem to crop up again and again for divers on Cozumel. Most are related to lodging. Making reservations in Mexico has always been a bit tricky. Although most hotel owners are honest and try to do a good job, we've heard enough stories about rooms going to the highest bidder—or dive boats suddenly being too full to accommodate everyone in a group—that we feel compelled to offer some advice on the matter.

Reservations made from the U.S. by a reputable dive travel specialist or tour wholesaler nearly always work out. Dive travel specialists account for a lot of business, and have much more leverage than an individual traveler does. A resort would take a serious financial risk by mistreating the clients of a dive travel specialist. Furthermore, dive packages are usually prepaid. Dive operators and hotels who work with dive travel specialists are assured that they will suffer no financial loss even if the client doesn't show up. There's no need to "overbook" (sell more rooms or boat slots than they have available).

On the other hand, people sometimes don't show up when they're expected. Their plans change, they miss their flights or taxis, and so forth. Overbooking has been one strategy for dealing with the potential loss of revenue. At worst, giving away an individual traveler's room or failing to provide a dive package is unlikely to cost the resort more than a shouting match at the front desk, and perhaps a protracted squabble with a credit card provider.

If you prefer to make your own individual reservations, ask around first to select a decent dive operator and a hotel with a good reputation. Confirm your reservations by fax or registered mail (especially if bearing checks). Pay with a credit card if at all possible so that you can look for reimbursement if the worst happens. Above all, bring copies of fax replies and/or receipts with you to present to the front desk.

Tipping

Tipping in Mexico is similar to tipping in the U.S. The range for excellent service is 15-20%, and the trades relying on tips are those traditional ones that cater to travelers (waiters and waitresses, cab drivers, hotel staff, dive guides, etc.). Be sure to check your hotel or restaurant bill to see if service is included (*servicio incluido*) in the charges; if it is, no tip is expected.

L. MARTIN

Cozumel's International Pier complex (two piers) hosts an ever-increasing stream of cruise ships, ferry boats to the mainland, and other commercial vessels. For your own safety, don't dive or swim near the piers.

Transportation

Flying Cozumel has a surprisingly busy international airport, with numerous direct flights from other parts of Mexico and the U.S. Flights from Europe are usually routed via the U.S. or Mexico City. There are direct flights on Continental and American from Houston and Miami, respectively, with many direct flights from other U.S. cities via these hubs. Mexicana has nonstops from Miami and direct flights from its hub in Mexico City. Aero Cozumel, run by Mexicana, with offices at Cozumel airport, operates flights between Cancún and Cozumel about every hour throughout the day.

Ferries Passenger ferries make a dozen runs daily from Playa del Carmen to Cozumel. A one-way trip takes about 30 minutes. Car ferries depart from Puerto Morelos daily (times subject to the season and weather conditions). The voyage takes 2½ - 4 hours.

Car Rentals Rental cars can be arranged by almost every hotel or condominium, but it is not uncommon to have every car on the island reserved. The best procedure is to reserve a rental car through an international company that is represented in the U.S. Most of the larger companies have an office at the airport; some also have offices at the luxury hotels. Driving is on the right-hand side of the road, with the likely possibility of arrest and detention in case of an accident, so be on the defensive and be sure to buy insurance. The larger hotels and a number of highly visible shops in town (within a block of the plaza) rent mopeds. You'll recognize them by their huge signs and the fleets of motor bikes parked in front. See the "Documents" section for further information on car rentals.

Taxis While you can rent a car to get to shore diving locations or to shops, taxis are abundant and very inexpensive, and you may find it convenient to leave the transportation to them. The cost of a taxi ride is fixed within town and along the hotel strip, and the prices are posted in each cab. If you want to go around to the eastern side of the island, though, renting a car is preferable; you'll want to stop to have a beach all to yourself, and you almost certainly won't be able to summon a cab to pick you up later. There are virtually no phones outside of town and the hotel strip, so before you go adventuring, tell someone where you're going, and make sure you can change a flat tire!

Foreign Exchange, Language, Dining & Shopping

Foreign Exchange Nearly all of the hotels, stores, and restaurants on the island are used to dealing with foreigners. In addition to the American divers, cruise liners dock at Cozumel nearly every day, disgorging thousands of tourists. Consequently, U.S. dollars are accepted nearly everywhere at very close to the official exchange rate. It's not really worth the trouble to try and get a few cents more by standing in line to exchange dollars at the bank unless you plan to spend a lot of money. Currency other than U.S. dollars or pesos may present problems, however, and a bank visit may be required. You can buy pesos at many banks and airports in the U.S. as well as in Mexico in case you want to get this out of the way in advance.

Language Even if your Spanish is rusty (or nonexistent) you'll have no problem getting what you need on the island. Cozumel may be the easiest place in Mexico to visit if you don't speak Spanish, although any attempts

La Turista: Avoiding and Treating It

Perhaps a word of advice on sanitation might be welcome here, given the cost of a diving vacation and the unhappiness of having to sit out a dive due to illness. Throughout most tropical countries (Mexico included), it's a good practice not to consume any water or ice cubes that have not been purified (ask for *agua purificado* or carbonated mineral water, *agua mineral con gaz*). You will also increase your chances of avoiding difficulties if you don't eat salads or uncooked vegetables, avoid frozen popsicle treats, peel all fruit, and bring a prescription antibiotic just in case.

If worse comes to worst and you catch Montezuma's revenge, there is a pharmacy (*farmacia*) within the large market-department store at the northeast corner of the plaza, and the pharmacy will generally dispense whatever you need, even drugs that are available only on prescription in the U.S., if you know what to ask for and how to use it. The paranoid diver (ourselves included) has his own doctor set up a medical kit before leaving home, taking into account the possibility of catching the *turista* on the road. Imodium is a very effective rapid treatment for the turista. It's available without a prescription in the U.S.

to communicate in Spanish (even high-school Spanish!) will be graciously received and encouraged.

Dining Most restaurants have menus in English and Spanish, and almost every restaurant, store, and hotel has someone on staff or within reach who speaks English. Restaurant dining therefore will present no unusual challenges to visiting divers. Seafood is the island specialty, and fresh conch, lobster, and fish are served proudly by most restaurants. Though temperatures remain warm all year, the dress style all over the island is diver-elegant (i.e., t-shirts or light sports clothes), and you won't need to take your tie or dinner jacket anywhere.

Shopping Most consumer goods such as canned or packaged food at markets are imported from the U.S. Consequently, don't expect any bargains on American products whatever the peso/dollar exchange rate may be. These goods are purchased with dollars and shipped from the U.S. into Mexico (picking up some taxes along the way). Gourmands note: the shops are used to catering to post-dive munchie fits, and most food stores sell Danish cookies, fancy Dutch and Swiss chocolate bars, and similar vital commodities. Make sure they aren't melted before leaving the store. We once had a heartbreaking experience on a sunny day with a pile of vital, emergency-use-only, raspberry-filled bittersweet candy bars . . .

L. MARTIN

The local economy is heavily dependent on divers and other tourists. The hand-crafted products found in shops or from individual craftsmen, such as this hammock maker, make excellent buys.

There are many Mexican souvenir items available, and the best buys may be had on these. As in other Mexican locations, high-quality sterling silver jewelry, handmade blankets, hammocks, serapes, carved onyx chess sets and figurines, and simulated pre-Columbian pottery are sold by most shops. *Caveat emptor* is the rule of thumb, although the stamp "sterling" on sil ver can almost always be relied on as its use is controlled by the Mexican government. Expect to bargain for souvenir-type items, with the original asking price perhaps double the final selling price, but don't bother haggling in any of the department stores or markets selling imported goods. Lots of souvenirs seem to be designed mainly for divers, such as carvings of sea creatures and turtle-shell combs, rings, and bracelets. Sea turtles are on the Endangered Species List for the U.S., however, and it is illegal to import any turtle-shell items into the States. Customs will seize them (and you, if you try to sneak them in) upon your return.

Documents

To get into Mexico you'll need some proof of citizenship (e.g. passport, birth certificate, voter's registration). Use of an official embossed-seal birth certificate or voter's registration must be accompanied by an official photo I.D. such as a state I.D. or driver's license. If you're bringing along any minors who are not accompanied by *both* parents, you must have a notarized, detailed letter from the absent parent or parents giving you permission to take the child into Mexico for a vacation.

On your arrival in Mexico, you'll be issued a Mexican Tourist Permit – a thin blue-and-pink document complete with signatures and rubber stamps. Don't lose it! You'll need the permit to leave Mexico, and may be asked to show it at any time by Mexican officials. When you leave Mexico, you'll turn in your Tourist Permit along with a departure tax (about US$13 as of this writing, but subject to increase) if you fly out. Note that some airline tickets include the departure tax in the fare. When you check in at the airport, ask the ticket agent to see if your departure tax is prepaid.

Driver's License If you plan to rent a car or moped, you'll need your home driver's license, as well as a major credit card or a giant wad of cash to show you can financially cover any damage to the vehicle.

C-Card Unless you have your diver's certification with you, you will not be able to rent tanks or charter boats. In other words, no card, no diving, no fun.

Diving in Cozumel

This book describes a number of popular spots and some that are less frequently dived but well worth seeing. Several shore dives are listed, and you will find that a few fine days can be spent diving from the shore for the cost of a taxi ride or two to entry and exit areas. Some reefs can be dived either from boat or shore, depending on how energetic (or lazy) you feel. Other reefs are best dived by boat.

The branch of the Gulf Stream that sweeps along the north/south-oriented island produces currents that range from barely perceptible to well over three knots. The farther offshore you go, the stronger the current (usually). The finest diving may be found on the crest of a near-vertical wall on the western shore of the island. Since this shore faces the mainland across a narrow channel, and away from the prevailing easterly winds, the weather here is usually much better for diving than on the eastern shore.

While there are spots on the eastern shore than can be dived during some conditions (e.g. strong west wind), these are not described in this guide because of the access difficulty and the typically marginal water states.

You should keep in mind that most of the reefs mentioned are very large, and this dive guide has been compiled to give an overview of what to expect. Consequently, it is possible to find deeper (or shallower) areas at each site, and currents may be much stronger or weaker than anticipated. Shoreline entry and exit spots can change with time, too. Your best source of information about any location will probably be local divers, especially those working for charter dive operators or shops, since they are familiar with the range of possibilities at each site.

Typical Dive Operations

Dive operators on Cozumel vary considerably with respect to their punctuality, the purity of their compressed air, the reliability of their boats,

Sponges grow under a ledge on the downcurrent side of a coral head.

and – most important – their concern for your safety. Some operators employ well-trained guides who are also diving instructors, while others may only hire local divers familiar with reef locations. Some boats carry first-aid kits, some carry oxygen, some have radios, and others don't. Some are affiliated with the B.M.M. recompression chamber, and some are not. Some use new tanks, while others use tanks that may not have been hydrostatically tested for fifteen years. Rental gear ranges from "donate-it-to-a-museum" vintage to near-new, depending on the operator.

The diving industry on Cozumel represents a vital economic resource to the island. Your business is anxiously sought by dive operators for this trip and for the next. You do have the right – and, perhaps, the responsibility – to demand first-class service from dive operators in exchange for your money. In the spirit of better, safer diving, we urge you to ask questions about those matters you consider important to you as a diver, and to reward only those operators you are satisfied with by giving your business to them. You can have a positive influence on the future of diving on Cozumel and at the same time increase your safety and enjoyment. For example, we tip a boat dive guide only if he treats our group courteously, provides a complete pre-dive briefing on the site and safety procedures, and keeps a watchful eye on the group in the water. No one likes to think about diving accidents, but consider, just for a moment, how an injury to you or your buddy would be handled, and don't be satisfied with vague answers.

Cozumel dive boats have evolved to modern, faster vessels, increasing comfort and safety for divers.

L. MARTIN

Many hotel piers make excellent entrance and exit points for shore dives.
Be sure to plan your dive carefully so you know exactly where the exit will be and
watch for boats when near or on the surface.

Dive Boats There are many dive boat operators on the island. Two types of boats are commonly used: open "flat-tops," with broad decks offer easy suiting up and entries and exits; and modern, high-powered run-abouts and small cabin cruisers are fast and stable even in rough seas. You may enjoy the roominess of the flat-tops, or instead just want to get to and from the dive site as fast as possible. You can make the choice if you ask the operators what kind of boats they run before booking trips. Rather than book all your diving with one operator, you might considered sampling several shops to see how they compare to one another. There are lots of differences.

Most of the operators offer two-tank trips, providing tanks, back-packs, and weights, with lunch included between dives. The lunch usually is served on San Francisco Beach, a beautiful white sand strip heavily patronized by local Mexican families was well as visiting divers. The most frequently visited part of San Francisco Beach has restrooms, restaurants and bars, live music, and good fun. Alternatively, some operators prefer a more remote section of the beach where charcoal-barbecued fish and isolation are the attractions.

Shore Diving If you are diving from the shore, you will find it extremely easy to rent tanks, backpacks, and weights at the many dive shops in town, or at the hotels. Most shops rent aluminum cylinders. Older cylinders holding 70 cubic feet at 3,000 psi are still common but many operators use newer 3,000 psi 80's, so look carefully before you rent. Hot, short fills unfortunately are pretty common on Cozumel, although less likely to occur at the larger shops. It's worth the trouble to gauge your rental tank before carrying it away from the shop. If you want to go diving after 5 p.m., plan ahead – most shops close about then.

Useful Dive Techniques

Typical conditions on the western side are calm seas but strong currents. Drift diving is the norm for boat diving in most locations. As in any open-water situation, you should always carry an audible signal device such as a whistle or a Dive Alert horn, and an additional device capable of being seen from far away, such as a flashing strobe or inflatable signal tube.

For boat dives, a "live boat" technique is generally used by charter boat captains, who follow divers' bubbles to greet them at the end of the dive. A dive guide is often provided at both ends of a group in order to keep divers together while on the reef and to aid pickup at the surface. Divers who rush ahead without seeing the reef, or those who lag behind (usually photographers) make it exceptionally difficult for the dive guide to keep the group together. Be sure to describe your previous experience, swimming abilities, and any special concerns to the divemaster or dive guides on the boat. Given the strong currents around Cozumel, we do not recommend that you rent a boat on your own without a local dive guide and captain. There are special skills required to operate a "live" boat safely around divers, and Cozumel's waters favor using professional operators only.

Be particularly careful about boat traffic when approaching the surface from below. Look and listen, and stay with your group. This isn't just theoretical advice. The model we used for this book is an active diving instructor on Cozumel. She was run over by a boat several years ago, and nearly lost her foot to a prop. When we returned to shoot the third edition, she had a very impressive scar on her ankle to show us!

For shore dives, an exit spot some distance down-current must be selected (and inspected) in advance, since it may be impossible to return to the starting point up-current. Booties, wetsuits and gloves are recommended to deal with ironshore (the sharp limestone pieces that can abrade tender flesh). Many hotel piers can serve as excellent starting and end spots for shore dives. They often feature ideal entrances and exits, such as concrete steps and ladders, and are generally placed in areas sheltered from strong currents. Transportation can be found easily at both the start and end of a dive at hotels. Taxis sometimes park at hotels, waiting for business, and the hotels can always call a taxi for you while you're dripping dry! Don't worry about carrying money with you to cover cabfare at the end of a dive; cabs will wait while you run inside your hotel to get your money.

If you are planning to dive from the shore, be sure not to swim any farther than your capabilities allow for a safe, easy return, and ask the local divers to help you to evaluate water conditions before jumping in. You should also bring along a dive flag on a float. Take this recommendation seriously. On a previous trip, this book's second author (Larry R. Martin) was arrested for diving from shore without a flag, and nearly had his dive gear confiscated. The usual current direction is parallel to shore from south to north, with speed increasing as you get farther offshore, but the current sometimes reverses direction and can occasionally take a seaward course. Before your dive, arrange with someone on shore to keep watch along the expected drift pathway and meet you at your exit point at a given time. That way, if you have any problems en route, help can be summoned promptly.

Cozumel may be enjoyed by divers with a wide range of skill levels. However, charter dive operators do not, at present, always separate experts from novices on boat dives. For wall dives in particular, an experienced guide will add considerably to your safety and comfort. For a beginner, to be dropped over a vertical wall in a strong current may be an exciting situation to say the least. Even for the pro there are a few surprises possible. For example, when high-velocity water runs into a coral buttress, zones of rapid upwelling and downwelling develop. Being caught in one of the down-slope currents is similar to being flushed in a gigantic toilet, and divers must be aware of their depths and surroundings at all times.

A little specialized practice on buoyancy control, drift-diving techniques, and deep-diving methods with a qualified instructor can go a very long way toward ensuring a pleasant, safe trip. This instruction should be arranged with the dive shop or charter operator before getting on the boat, however, as dive guides may have their hands full and not be able to offer any instruction without prior appointments. Furthermore, the majority of dive guides on the island are just that – guides – and are not diving instructors. Again, set up any instruction you may need in advance.

L. MARTIN

These large knobby coral polyps are cavernous star coral. They come in a
variety of colors and are a principal reef builder.

Cozumel Diving Recommendations

The following recommendations apply when currents are minimal or nonexistent during a dive. More current calls for more caution:

Inexperienced divers should never place themselves in any situation where loss of buoyancy control could result in rapid depth increases. This translates as advice to keep away from walls (that is, near-vertical or vertical dropoffs). Diving on or near walls is safe only for advanced divers, or for intermediate divers under proper supervision. Gradual dropoffs present less hazard, and diving on or below the lip of these dropoffs (slopes less steep than 45°) should be within the capabilities of well-supervised novices. The word "supervised" should be understood to mean that a diver is under the direct supervision of a qualified instructor or divemaster. These recommendations should be taken in a conservative sense, keeping in mind the old adage about there being old divers and bold divers but few old bold divers.

Penetration of wrecks, diving in caverns or caves, or diving below a depth of 100 feet (30 meters) is suitable only for advanced divers with specialized training in these skills. Diving below a depth of 130 feet (40 meters) is outside the realm of sport diving.

L. MARTIN

Pisces Rating System for Dives & Divers

The dive sites in this book are rated according to the following diver skill level rating system. These are not absolute ratings but apply to divers at a particular time, diving at a particular place.

Please be aware that *any* dive site discussed in this book can be hazardous, depending on prevailing conditions. Many of Cozumel's dive sites include shallow areas, as well as deeper areas and dropoffs. Furthermore, the dive sites also vary in their exposure to current. Both current and depth need to be taken into account for every dive. A suitable dive for a novice when the water is still may be unsafe for an advanced diver when current velocity is too high.

Novice: A novice diver generally fits the following profile:
- ◆ basic scuba certification from an internationally recognized certifying agency
- ◆ dives infrequently (less than one trip a year)
- ◆ logged fewer than 25 total dives
- ◆ little or no experience diving in similar waters and conditions
- ◆ dives no deeper than 60 feet (18 meters)
- * *A novice diver should be accompanied by an instructor or divemaster on all dives*

Intermediate: An intermediate diver generally fits the following profile:
- ◆ may have participated in some form of continuing diver education
- ◆ logged between 25 and 100 dives
- ◆ dives no deeper than 130 feet (40 meters)
- ◆ has been diving within the last six months in similar waters and conditions

Advanced: An advanced diver generally fits the following profile:
- ◆ advanced certification
- ◆ has been diving for more than 2 years; logged over 100 dives
- ◆ has been diving within the last six months in similar waters and conditions

Regardless of skill level, you should be in good physical condition and know your limitations. If you are uncertain as to which category you fit, ask the advice of a local dive instructor. You will have to decide yourself, of course, if you are capable of making any particular dive depending on your level of training, recency of experience, physical condition, and on the water conditions at the site. Water conditions, topography, and exit and entry points can change at any time, even during a dive. It is *your* responsibility to determine whether or not any particular dive is within your capabilities, and whether conditions are safe when you make that dive.

Cozumel Dive Sites

	Good Snorkeling	Novice	Intermediate	Advanced
1 Paraíso Reef North			✓	✓
2 The Junkyard (formerly Airplane Flats)	✓	✓	✓	✓
3 Paraíso Reef South	✓	✓	✓	✓
4 Chankanab	✓	✓	✓	✓
5 Beachcomber Cavern				✓
6 Tormentos Reef			✓	✓
7 Yocab Reef			✓	✓
8 El Paso del Cedral Reef			✓	✓
9 Tunich				✓
10 Cardona Reef		✓	✓	✓
11 San Francisco Reef			✓	✓
12 Santa Rosa Reef			✓	✓
13 Palancar Reef			✓	✓
14 Punta Sur				✓
15 Colombia Reef			✓	✓
16 Maracaibo Reef				✓
17 Colombia Shallows	✓	✓	✓	✓
18 Sand Diver's Secret	✓	✓	✓	✓

Dive Site Icons

The symbols at the beginning of the dive site descriptions provide a quick summary of some of the following conditions present at the site:

 Good snorkeling or free diving site

 Vertical wall or drop-off

 Drift dive

 Deep dive (100 feet/30 meters or more). Only for divers experienced in deep-diving techniques.

 Cave or caverns. Only experienced cave divers should explore inner cave areas.

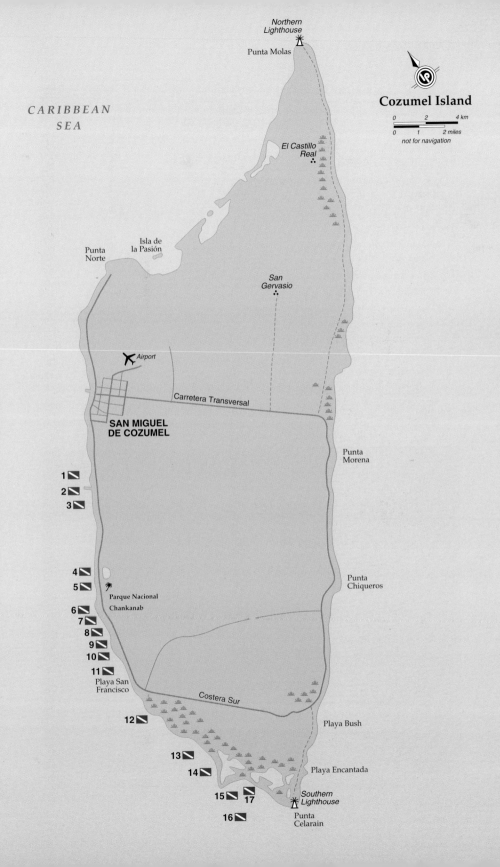

CARIBBEAN
SEA

Northern
Lighthouse
Punta Molas

Cozumel Island

0   2   4 km
0   1   2 miles
not for navigation

El Castillo
Real

Isla de
la Pasión

Punta
Norte

San
Gervasio

Airport

Carretera Transversal

SAN MIGUEL
DE COZUMEL

Punta
Morena

1
2
3

4
5

Parque Nacional
Chankanab

Punta
Chiqueros

6
7
8
9
10
11

Playa San
Francisco

Costera Sur

12

Playa Bush

13

14

Playa Encantada

15
17

Southern
Lighthouse

16

Punta
Celarain

1 Paraíso Reef North

Paraíso (Paradise) Reef North is a series of backbone-like strips of coral running parallel to the shore. The series can be intersected by swimming perpendicular to the shore out to a depth of about 40-50 feet (12-14 meters). If you exceed this depth you've missed the reef and gone too far, and you should turn around and head back toward shore. Paraíso Reef North lies just seaward of the sand flat that is marked at its shoreward edge by the sunken airplane (see the description of the Junkyard). To find Paraíso North, swim from the plane straight offshore toward the wall, bearing slightly to the right (northward). It is about a five-minute swim from the plane.

The reef consists of large coral heads and sponges up to 6 feet (2 meters) in

Typical Depth Range:
   40-50 feet (12-15 meters)
Typical Current Conditions:
   Light to moderate, occasionally strong
Access:
   La Ceiba Hotel or via the small beach cove
   at Crown Princess Sol Caribe Hotel
Expertise Required:
   Intermediate

diameter. Large schools of iridescent blue chromis fishes form clouds above the reef, and if you hunt carefully around the sandy bases of the big coral heads you may catch a glimpse of the blue-, white-, and yellow-

Bar jacks are often seen over sand near slopes and dropoffs.

L. MARTIN

This giant anemone is surrounded by algae
(small, green, crunchy feeling "wingnuts").

striped splendid toadfish. Paraíso North is not large – a few hundred feet long – and is probably best visited as part of a longer dive, perhaps starting at this reef and proceeding inward to end near the airplane.

Paraíso North is far enough offshore to be subject to the influence of strong currents, and if you're headed to or from this reef you may have to correct for drift. If you're carried northward by the current you will find the handiest exit at the Crown Princess Sol Caribe pier. If you're carried southward, stay on the bottom, avoid the area of the International Pier, and exit at La Ceiba Hotel. There is often boat traffic between Paraíso North, the Sol Caribe, and La Ceiba, so if you're on or near the surface you should keep alert and be prepared to get out of the way of vessels that may not see or avoid you.

2 The Junkyard (formerly Airplane Flats)

The Junkyard (formerly Airplane Flats) is an area that stretches from in front of La Ceiba Hotel on the south to just north of the Crown Princess Sol Caribe Hotel. Most of the terrain is rather flat, but there's a lot to see. Snorkelers will find this an excellent spot to see fish and gorgonians (sea fans). There is also wreckage of an old airplane (placed here as a prop for the movie *Survive* by film director Ramon Bravo in 1977) that makes a dramatic backdrop for photographs. Unfortunately, the area is also littered with old tires, barrels, pipes, cables, and other large pieces of junk. If it ever gets cleaned up, we'll change its name in this book back to "Airplane Flats." Snorkelers can rent gear from the full-service dive stores at most of the hotels along the waterfront.

Due to easy access and lights at the hotels and docks, this is a near-perfect

Typical Depth Range
   10-35 feet (3-10 meters)
Typical Current Conditions: Light
Access: La Ceiba Hotel, or via the small beach
   cove at the Crown Princess Sol Caribe Hotel
Expertise Required: Novice

site for night diving. If there's any current running, you might consider jumping in at the up-current end of the site (usually, but not always, La Ceiba) and exiting at the down-current site (usually the Sol Caribe) to save yourself some swimming.

In any event, don't dive or swim south of La Ceiba Hotel, and stay well clear of the International Pier complex. The piers are illegal to approach closely due to the hazards presented by cruise liners,

G. LEWBEL

The Junkyard is the easily accessed site of an old airplane used as a movie prop.
Nowadays, not much of the plane is intact, and piles of junk have been dumped here.

ferry boats, and other vessels. For that matter, quite a few boats pick up and drop off divers at the various piers bordering the Junkyard. Keep your eyes open on the surface, and don't ascend without checking for approaching traffic. The hand you save could be your own!

Near shore, there are some elkhorn coral heads, though the best formations were battered by a major hurricane in 1988. Long-spined sea urchins are common around these coral heads. Be careful not to touch them or step on them. Beds of

The Mexican federal government made the western shore of Cozumel a national marine park to help protect the many unusual species found here, such as the splendid Cozumel toadfish.

gorgonians begin at a depth of around 10 feet (3 meters) and continue seaward on a shallow shelf, which is ideal for snorkelers. At night, basket stars are frequently seen spread out on top of gorgonians, feeding in the dark. There are also big open areas on the shelf with a few small coral heads. These areas are excellent places to look for large rainbow parrotfishes, especially when the sun is low in the late afternoon. You'll see them feeding on the bottom, picking at plants and chunks of coral. The shallows are patrolled by territorial damselfishes that despite their diminutive size are inclined to nip at offending divers.

The shelf breaks at the edge of a sand flat about 30 to 40 feet (9 to 13 meters) deep, where a low-profile coral reef replaces the gorgonian beds a few hundred feet from shore. The most characteristic species are leaf or ribbon corals. This reef is an ideal first dive for training purposes, or a good warmup dive for novices and rusty veterans. There is enough open space over the sand to practice buoyancy control, and enough fish action to keep the

A patch of red encrusting sponge is growing over this mountainous star coral.

dive interesting. The coral is not in very good shape due to heavy traffic and storm damage, but you'll find plenty of things to see. The fish are accustomed to handouts, so don't be surprised if you're mobbed by Bermuda chub or sergeant majors. Due to the large amount of trash on the bottom, keep your eyes open and beware of sharp or entangling objects.

A bit farther out, you'll find the remains of an old twin-engine prop plane. At this time, it lies on sandy bottom directly out from La Ceiba Hotel in about 40 feet (12 meters) of water. Storms have moved it around a bit, and will continue to do so, but it usually is marked with a surface buoy by the hotels because it's such a popular dive site. Be careful not to get snagged in any lines, and look out for sharp edges. Many fish have made it their home, and octopus are not uncommon. Its surface remains fairly clean due to the scraping bites of parrotfish, whose toothmarks can be seen on the metal along with the graffiti of thoughtless divers. Also, look for purple patches of sergeant major eggs on the plane. They'll be guarded by expectant – and aggressive – parents.

3 Paraíso Reef South

Paraíso (Paradise) Reef South consists of two long ridges of coral running parallel to shore end-to-end, at depths of about 35-45 feet (11-12 meters), surrounded by sand. It is frequently visited by charter boats as a second dive after a deeper wall dive. It is also a favorite among dive operators for night dives, since it is a short boat ride from most hotels, and is fairly shallow. It may also be reached easily from the shore, but ongoing construction at this time makes that inadvisable. It's a bit deep for most skin divers, but the nearshore ridge is a good reef to snorkel over and watch scuba divers. Look out for boat traffic!

Paraíso Reef South is home to many tame fish that have been fed by dive guides. If you're hoping to see large, bizarre filefish, or French and gray angels within arms' reach, you probably won't be disappointed. The coral formations are medium-sized and this entire reef is relatively low in profile. The small crevices at the bases of the coral heads shelter many squirrelfish during the daytime, and serve as "toeholds" for the six-foot-long

Typical Depth Range:
35-45 feet (11-14 meters)
Typical Current Conditions: Moderate
Access: Boat
Expertise Required: Novice

Tame fish such as this French grunt are a photographer's delight at Paraíso Reef South.

L. MARTIN

Red and orange sponges splash the sides of a
coral head with their brilliant color.

(2 meters) sea cucumbers that stretch out on the sand at night to feed. The reef is ideal for photographers, since depth control on the fairly level bottom is far simpler than on any of the walls. If you're planning to make a wall dive during your stay on Cozumel, you'll find that when the current is running, Paraíso South is a good place to get some experience in drift diving techniques over level bottom before you hit the dropoffs.

If the current is running to the north, drift along the coral ridge with it. The first ridge is several hundred yards long, and ends abruptly in sand at its northernmost point. If your air and bottom time permit, continue swimming toward the north, but angle to your left (westward or seaward) about 30° when you leave the first ridge. You will come to the southern tip of the second ridge within minute or two. The second section parallels the shore, but slightly seaward of the first, and is about the same in length. The second section also ends in sand at its northern tip. There is a small third section farther north and more seaward still, but it is near the site of the new pier and should be avoided due to vessel traffic. If the current is running to the south, ask to be dropped on the northern tip of the northern ridge, and do the dive just described in reverse.

4 Chankanab

Chankanab ("Chankanaab" on some maps) is one of the most popular shore dives on the island. This site is used for training purposes and for "rusty" divers to refresh their skills before diving the deeper sites. There's a beautiful botanical garden here, too.

Chankanab boasts facilities for gear rental and air fills, and is a popular weekend location for island residents due to new picnic facilities and shops selling snacks. It's also one of the more common sites for moped crashes due to the large speed bumps installed in the road, so be careful.

Typical Depth Range: 10-35 feet (nearshore coral heads) (3-11 meters)
Typical Current Conditions: Light
Access:
Walk into the water down concrete steps
Expertise Required: Novice

Concrete steps and ladders provide extremely easy access to the ocean. The bottom immediately adjacent is about 10 feet (3 meters) deep. There are large schools of tame fish – especially grunts and snappers – that can nearly always be found under large ledges within a few yards of the steps. Photographers will find these fish cooperative and very used to divers (they've appeared on several posters!).

The area just offshore has tall patch reefs separated by sand channels. The bases of the coral heads are especially good spots to find spotted drums and jacknife fishes. Local tourist interests have placed a small wrecked fishing boat on the bottom just a few hundred feet off the steps (look for the mast sticking out of the water), and an assortment of old cannons and anchors on the sand flats near shore. Unfortunately, Chankanab is usually mobbed by groups of tourists from the cruise ships who snorkel en masse. Experienced divers may want to avoid Chankanab, although photographers may enjoy watching the chaos. Chankanab also offers easy access to Beachcomber Cavern (see next site), and is the present location of Cozumel's famous "Christ of the Abyss" statue.

Lush gorgonians populate shallow sandy areas where rocky substrate is available for attachment.

5 Beachcomber Cavern

Just to the south of the main entrances/exits at Chankanab are several entrances to a large cavern that lead to a cave, which penetrates the island for an unknown distance. The site is often called Beachcomber Cavern in memory of a fine seafood restaurant (the Beachcomber) that used to sit above the entrances. The restaurant has since been removed, but the site can be found easily without this landmark.

Typical Depth Range:
   10-35 feet (3-11 meters)
Typical Current Conditions:
   Access and cavern entrance, light to none; inner portion, unknown
Access: Via Chankanab, or by boat
Expertise Required: Advanced

To get to the entrances, swim on the surface a few hundred feet south (parallel to shore) from Chankanab, staying close to shore until you are facing a large channel-like cut in the shore. Face the shore and you will see a narrow boat channel about 20 feet (6 meters) wide and about 10-15 feet (3-5 meters) deep.

It's open on the seaward side and comes to an abrupt end about 50 feet (15 meters) in from the shoreline. You'll be looking at the mouth of it from the seaward side. The main entrance (and exit) to the cavern is just to the left of the cut, on the north side of the rocks that mark

L. MARTIN

A mass of silver fingerlings boils out of the entrance to Beachcomber Cavern.

The Green Mirror

This cavern is famous for a peculiar hydrologic phenomenon that can result in some amazing photographs. Fresh water has saturated the island and, in some locations such as this, seeps back into the sea as if from a sponge. The fresh water is usually colder than the ocean, but it is so much less dense than salt water that it floats on top if protected from turbulence. The cavern provides this protection, allowing a *reverse thermocline* with warmer water below colder water. The fresh water usually forms a brilliant green-colored band a few feet thick on the surface. Sometimes it even produces a mirror-like reflective layer three or four feet (one meter) beneath the surface. Try to see it on your way in before your bubbles and turbulence have disturbed the layer. It's most visible from within the cavern, looking outward through the entrances. After you leave the outer cavern exits you can feel the cold, fresh water on the surface, and see the shimmering mixing layer where the sale and fresh water combine.

the northern edge of the cut. The main entrance is shaped like an inverted triangle, about 10-15 feet (3-5 meters) on each a side. There are several alternative entrances and exits on the north side of the boat channel. Most of these openings are large enough for several divers to pass through side-by-side, but if there are any waves or swells you should stay out of the channel to avoid getting beaten against the ironshore (eroded limestone) by sloshing water.

The main entrance to the outer cavern is usually filled with small, silvery fish that form a solid-looking curtain from surface to bottom and from side to side. The curtain will part dramatically as you swim through. Both the main and alternative entrances open into the outer cavern, which consists of a large central room about 20-30 feet (6-10 meters) in diameter and about 10 feet (3 meters) high, supported by numerous pillars. The outer cavern ceiling does not enclose any airspaces, but has some small holes (too small for a diver to fit through) that allow

Warning!

Specialized training and equipment for cavern or cave diving techniques are essential to enter any cavern or cave safely. If you do not have this training and equipment, stay outside the entrances. If you bring a flashlight to the entrances, you will be able to see nearly all of the outer cavern without having to go inside yourself.

The cave has not yet been fully mapped, although a few divers have penetrated it for some distance. Due to lack of information about the inner portion, the authors must recommend strongly against entering any sections of the cave except for the outer cavern, that is, the area in which certified, trained cave divers can remain within sight of and immediate reach (one breath) of an exit to the outside. Diving the inner portion should be done only by experts equipped and trained for exploratory cave diving.

L. MARTIN

A squirrelfish lurks beneath a sponge-covered outcrop.

beams of sunlight to get through. Several dark, smaller side rooms open onto this central room, and tunnels lead to the inner portion of the cave. The outer cavern and the inner cave have areas of soft, silty bottom that can be resuspended in the water by swimming, so be very careful not to stir up the bottom or you'll lose your visibility! Within the dark cavern you'll be able to see a variety of nocturnal fish (glassy sweepers, bigeyes, glasseye snappers) and possibly a large grouper or two taking a nap during the day. A few urchins sometimes hide near the entrances in the shadows, so use your lights before touching down.

6 Tormentos Reef

This reef is similar in many respects to Yocab and El Paso del Cedral reefs. The coral heads on Tormentos Reef are a bit taller (10 feet, or 3 meters) than those on Yocab, and a bit lower than those on El Paso del Cedral, but the fauna and topography are comparable. The back sides of the coral heads provide resting places out of the strong south-to-north prevailing current, and you'll find endless subjects for macro photography on the undersides of the heads. Lobsters and

Typical Depth Range:
  50-70 feet (15-20 meters)
Typical Current Conditions: Strong
Access: Boat
Expertise Required: Intermediate

nurse sharks are also abundant in the crevices on the north sides of the coral heads. Tormentos is a great place to see

L. MARTIN

The back sides of coral formations provide refuge
from the prevailing current at Tormentos.

L. MARTIN

Large old sponges are prevalent at high current sites.

big black groupers, smaller yellowmouth or scamp groupers, barracudas, and pairs of white-spotted filefishes. The white sand dunes inshore of Tormentos are spectacular, too.

Tormentos Reef is long enough so that you're likely to burn a full tank before you run out of coral. If you lift off the bottom into the current, you'll usually be carried along without putting any effort into swimming. To take a break, just duck behind a coral head and hug the sand on the downstream side. For your safety stay with your fellow divers (especially your dive buddy) and your dive guide.

7 Yocab Reef

Yocab (also spelled "Yucab" on some maps) is sometimes a second dive of the day on boat dives, as it is possible to see a good deal of the reef without exceeding 50 feet (15 meters). Yocab is strongly recommended to those who like drift diving. The reef runs parallel to the current direction and is surrounded by brilliant white sand. Large ripple marks can be attributed to the strong current that usually sweeps over the area from south to north. Large coral heads stick out of the sand to a height of 5-10 feet

Typical Depth Range:
  50-70 feet (15-20 meters)
Typical Current Conditions:
  Moderate to strong
Access: Boat
Expertise Required: Intermediate

(2-3 meters). On the down-current sides of these heads, divers will find some refuge from the current and a truly marvelous

L. MARTIN

Smooth trunkfish and an abundance of other reef creatures are found hiding from the prevailing current in the undercuts of Yocab Reef. The current generally runs from south to north, and the northern sides of the large coral mounds are marked by scoured-out tunnels, arches, and caves.

L. MARTIN

Coral heads on Yocab Reef extend 5-10 feet above the sand bottom, which is about 50 feet deep. Many of the heads exhibit a dazzling array of colorful growth.

collection of animals hiding out in the backwaters. The down-current ends of coral heads have been sculptured and weathered by sand scour, and many caves and ledges harbor schools of fish, large lobsters, crabs, and the like. Photographers will probably be frustrated by the current in most spots, but may shoot down "on the deck" in the eaves of the coral heads. Fish drift along with divers when the current is strong. Very large white-spotted and scrawled filefish frequent Yocab Reef.

Yocab Reef comes to a distinct northern end, marked by a huge coral mound at about 60 feet (18 meters). Beyond this mound the sand slopes rapidly downward toward the wall, and divers will want to make their ascents on sighting this mount at the tip of the reef. As with other drift dives, it is important to stay together with your guides or divemasters, since charter boats usually drift above groups, following their bubbles and picking up all divers together at the end of the dive.

8 El Paso del Cedral Reef

El Paso del Cedral Reef is a long, backbone-style reef similar to Yocab and Tormentos. All three reefs have large, relatively low-profile coral heads along a ridge that separates a shallow sand flat from a deeper sand flat. The terrain on El Paso del Cedral is higher in profile, but there are more sandy stretches between coral heads at El Paso del Cedral. The tops of the coral heads lie in the 40-50-foot (12-15 meter) depth range, with bases in sand on the seaward side at closer to 60 feet. Most of the coral heads are in a fairly straight line with respect to prevailing currents, meaning that you can ride the flow and see most of the reef. After you think you've run out of coral, a gentle left turn across the sand will take you over an additional section of coral.

Typical Depth Range:
  40-60 feet (12-18 meters)
Typical Current Conditions: Strong
Access: Boat
Expertise Required: Intermediate

This reef boasts very large schools of porkfish, French grunts, cottonwick, and snappers that rest out of the current in small caverns and notches on the north, down-current side of the coral heads. As at Tormentos and Yocab, it's very important to stay with your buddy, your group, and your dive guides. If you slip out of the current and everyone else is still drifting with it, they'll blow downstream out of sight in a few seconds, and vice versa.

Schools of bluestriped grunts are common at El Paso del Cedral.

9 Tunich

Tunich lies along the edge of Punta Tunich, between Punta Tormentos and San Francisco Beach. Tunich is almost always washed by strong currents. Expect an exciting, high-velocity drift dive along the rim of a dropoff, where currents are usually strongest. Unlike many of the more traditional reef dives on Cozumel, Tunich does not have steep buttress and groove coral formations. A beautiful white sand flat at about 60-80 feet (16-24 meters) borders a fairly gentle slope that falls off at around 45° toward the abyss. The edge of the dropoff is an excellent place to see

Typical Depth Range:
    60 feet (18 meters) minimum to unlimited (dropoff)
Typical Current Conditions: Strong
Access: Boat
Expertise Required: Advanced

schools of bar jacks and larger pelagics such as turtles and eagle rays. Thousands of other fish are usually there, including huge rainbow parrots and groupers, and

French angelfish are easily spotted on the open slope at Tunich.

Large, north-facing basket sponges are a prime feature at Tunich.

more queen triggerfish than you're likely to see anywhere else.

The main attraction at Tunich is the huge basket sponges. Why do all their cavities face toward the north, away from the current? A basket sponge draws water in through its outside surface, extracts oxygen and nutrients from the water, adds carbon dioxide and wastes, and dumps the filtered water out the central cavity. The cavity faces down-current so that water that has already been filtered can be carried away, and the current at Tunich nearly always runs toward the north. Other kinds of low-profile sponges are also common at Tunich. Look for big, flat brown patches up to 10 feet (3 meters) across, with small siphons sticking up to pump exhaled water away. These flat sponges, in particular, should not be touched; they can produce instant "sponge rash" and itching.

10 Cardona Reef

Cardona Reef is located a short distance north of San Francisco Reef, too far offshore for a beach dive. It is a good choice for a second boat dive, since most boat operators stop for lunch at nearby San Francisco Beach after visiting Palancar, Santa Rosa, or Colombia. It's a very worthwhile spot, too, if you've already seen enough parrotfishes and giant coral heads for the time being. Cardona might be con-

Typical Depth Range:
  20-45 feet (6-14 meters)
Typical Current Conditions: Light
Access: Boat
Expertise Required: Novice

sidered a connoisseur's reef, mainly interesting to divers looking for unusual

G. LEWBEL

Barred cardinalfish hide in a colony of pillar coral at Cardona Reef.

The undersides of many of the ledges at Cardona Reef are covered with green algae. Nocturnal fish such as squirrelfish and glass sweepers often hide in the dark recesses beneath these ledges during the day.

species of fish. Bring a flashlight on this dive.

Cardona is a low-profile reef that has relatively few big coral heads and is better known for its long ledges and overhangs. Most of these ledges parallel the shoreline, forming a series of ridges.

If you're used to diving in cold water where there are a lot of algae and you've been wondering where the plants are on coral reefs, look under these ledges. Your flashlight will help you find bright green, wingnut-shaped algae hanging down in areas of reduced light.

Nocturnal Fishes by Day

The ledges at Cardona Reef provide shelter for some very large schools of nocturnal fish that hide under the overhangs. As a general rule, you can recognize nocturnal fish by two characteristics: first, they're hiding in caves and other dark places during the daytime; and second, they have big eyes with large pupils for effective night vision. Look for the hatchet-shaped glassy sweepers, the red-and-silver-barred glasseye snappers, and a variety of squirrelfishes. Cardinalfishes are also easy to find at Cardona, though they often hide among the spines of sea urchins. If you're taking pictures, you'll probably be able to get close enough to these small, beautiful fishes for a good strobe-lit shot, since many of the ledges are very large and roomy enough to lie beneath.

11 San Francisco Reef

San Francisco Reef is located directly offshore from San Francisco Beach. It consists of a fairly low-profile coral strip on the lip of a dropoff. If you have never made a wall drift dive, San Francisco Reef might be a good one to start with, since the edge of the dropoff is shallower than many of the other walls on Cozumel. In some places, the lip is as shallow as 20 feet (6 meters), though 50-60 feet (15-18 meters) is more typical. Even if you have lots of experience on walls, you'll really enjoy the extra bottom time you can get on this reef by staying shallow.

The reef is an excellent spot to see filefish, angelfish, trumpetfish, and other common reef species. It is also known for its sun anemones, which look like beds of small green grapes up to a foot across. The many

Typical Depth Range:
  20-60 feet (6-18 meters), but near a wall (depth unlimited)
Typical Current Conditions:
  Moderate to strong
Access: Boat
Expertise Required: Intermediate

nooks and crannies on San Francisco Reef shelter large lobsters, and you can often find bigeye, sweepers, and other nocturnal fish hiding in the crevices during the daytime. If you stray off the reef and over to the west, you'll be looking down into the dropoff; the white sand to the east is a good place for stingrays and conch.

A dive light will reveal spectacular colors beneath the overhangs.

12 Santa Rose Reef

Santa Rosa Reef shares a number of features with Palancar, Colombia, and the other coral buttress areas on the lip of the dropoff. It has tall columns of coral with vertical walls cut by channels which slope from the white sand bottom on their shoreward side down near-vertical, terraced canyons on their seaward side. As on the other buttress reefs, enormous plate corals, mammoth-sized sea

Typical Depth Range:
  50 feet (15 meters) minimum to unlimited (wall)
Typical Current Conditions:
  Moderate to strong
Access: Boat
Expertise Required: Intermediate

L. MARTIN

The wall at Santa Rosa is riddled with caves, grottos, and tunnels that are among the best on the island. The insides of these are often home to spectacular sponges.

fans, and spectacular sponges are common at Santa Rosa. The best diving is along the seaward faces of the buttresses, where divers can look down into blue depths and up along sheer cliff sides. Santa Rosa does differ from the other reefs in the diversity and quality of its caverns and grottos, though. If you want photographs or views of divers silhouetted in the mouths of caves or dropping through narrow slots between walls, this is your reef. Tame, hand-fed groupers are common here, too.

Santa Rosa Reef is known for strong currents, so drift diving is the norm. Be sure to monitor your own depth and time, because other divers may follow different dive profiles up and down the walls. Stay together with your dive guides or divemasters and with your group, as "live" boating is typical and you will all be picked up (ideally in a group) down-current from your starting spot.

13 Palancar Reef

Palancar Reef, the most famous on the island, is renowned for its towering coral buttresses. Similar in topography to Colombia Reef, Palancar is a long stretch of apartment-house-sized columns reaching as shallow as 30-40 feet (10-12 meters) in some areas but anchored on the edge of a vertical dropoff. Between the columns are white sand channels and caves on the sheer sides of the buttresses. It is possible to stay shallow at Palancar by not descending between buttresses or along the seaward faces, but most of the diving is along the outer wall.

Typical Depth Range:
  40 feet (12 meters) minimum to unlimited (wall)
Typical Current Conditions:
  Moderate to strong
Access: Boat
Expertise Required: Intermediate

An especially popular area of Palancar, called the Horseshoe (*la Herradura*), has been the subject of many photographic studies and posters. Another excellent area for a second dive is Palancar Gardens, which has miniature buttresses, canyons, and terraces, with dropoffs starting as shallow as 30 feet (10 meters). It is not possible to "see Palancar" in one dive or twenty, since the reef is tremendous in size, and charter operators frequently visit different areas of Palancar to provide variety for their clients. If you take pot luck, you won't be disappointed.

Strong currents sweep the area, and most boats operate unanchored, dropping divers off upstream of the dive site and picking them up at the other end. Stay together with your group and with your guides or divemasters to facilitate pickup once on the surface. As with any other wall dive, be sure to monitor your depth and time carefully.

14 Punta Sur

Punta Sur lies near the southern end of Cozumel, and is deeper than most wall dives on the island. Along the crest of the dropoff, there are large buttress formations of coral with caverns and channels similar to those at Santa Rosa. The tops of the formations reach 60 feet (18 meters) or so at the shallowest, but most of the good scenery lies below 80 feet (24 meters) on the face of the wall. The bases of the buttresses grade steeply into a sandy slope at depths too great for sport diving. The inshore sides of the buttresses rest on a deep sand flat (120-130 feet). Punta Sur has many caverns and tunnels penetrating the wall. The best known of

Typical Depth Range:
  100 feet (30 meters) to unlimited (wall)
Typical Current Conditions: Strong
Access: Boat
Expertise Required: Advanced

these is the Devil's Throat, which has become a popular (and dangerous) dive. Be aware that it is suitable only for trained, certified cave divers. The Devil's Throat requires penetration of a very deep, lightless passageway in a full "overhead" environment, without immediate access to the surface. Much of Punta Sur looks like a single long row of apartment buildings rising sharply on both seaward and inshore sides. The inshore sand flat spills over between the buttresses and flows down the dropoff, producing beautiful sand "waterfalls" and rivers.

This dive site is rapidly developing a reputation as one of the best places to find pelagic fishes such as sharks, horse-eye jacks, and eagle rays. Too deep for most divers, its coral and sponges have not yet felt the impact of careless knees and misplaced fins. With any luck, it will remain the province of very experienced divers, who (presumably) will have the necessary buoyancy control and diving skills to keep it in pristine condition.

Huge towering buttresses with large caverns are typical of Punta Sur.

L. MARTIN

L MARTIN

The Punta Sur wall: deep and steep!

15 Colombia Reef

Colombia Reef is one of the great coral buttress areas located along the lip of the dropoff toward the southern end of the island. Huge pillars of coral loom over white sand on the shoreward side and slope downward on the seaward side to successive terraces below. The tops of the pillars are mostly in the 60-70 foot (18-20 meter) range, while the narrow passageways and channels between them open onto the nearly vertical faces of the seaward side. You will find gigantic plate corals and huge sponges interspersed with anemones, gorgonian sea fans, and a wide variety of other attached organisms. Many fish live among the pillars and in the holes, caves, and crevices formed by the reef. Photographers will probably want to set up for wide-angle work, at least on a first dive, as the three-dimensional relief of Colombia Reef is second to none in the world.

The typical boat dive on Colombia Reef will be a drift dive, since strong currents prevail here. Some protection from water movement can be had on the backside of pillars and in channels, but divers can expect to cover quite a distance on one tank. As on all other wall dives, your selection of depth can range from the tops of the pillars to whatever your own judgment (and your guide) will permit. Your boat will probably operate unanchored, picking your group up at the end of the dive, so be sure to stay together with your dive guides or divemasters and the rest of your group. It's a long way to shore! Current direction on Colombia is quite variable, and large eddies and swirls are typical.

Typical Depth Range:
  60 feet (18 meters) minimum to unlimited (wall)

Typical Current Conditions:
  Moderate to strong

Access: Boat

Expertise Required: Intermediate

G. LEWBEL

Large gorgonians line the wall near the lip of the dropoff at Colombia Reef.

16 Maracaibo Reef

Maracaibo Reef is a deep reef at the southern tip of the island. If you want to dive Maracaibo, you'll probably have to get together with enough people to charter a boat and captain for the day (rather than ride on an "open" boat). In general, the captains on the slower boats will refuse to dive Maracaibo, since the

Typical Depth Range:
  100 feet (30 meters) to unlimited (wall)
Typical Current Conditions: Strong
Access: Boat
Expertise Required: Advanced

L. MARTIN

Pay particular attention to your instruments on Maracaibo. It's all deep!

run there and back takes a full day from town. The newer resorts near Punta Sur provide much faster access. All members of your party should be advanced, very experienced divers trained in deep-diving techniques. Due to its location, Maracaibo is less protected from weather and the ride there is often wet and rough, so if you're prone to seasickness you might sit this one out.

Maracaibo is a buttress reef, with the inshore edges of most buttresses at depths of 100 feet (30 meters) or more. The offshore wall lip is at least 120 feet (36 meters) deep in some locations, so watch your depth gauge! The coral formations of Maracaibo resemble the other large dropoff wall reefs (e.g. Palancar, Santa Rosa, Colombia), with tunnels and caves and vertical walls interspersed with broad sand channels. Very large buttresses are typical of Maracaibo. It's not worth the trouble to get to Maracaibo just to see coral, however. You can see spectacular coral and sponges at the other reefs more easily, less expensively, and with a shorter boat ride.

Shark Watching, Maybe!

Many of the divers that go to Maracaibo go to see sharks. Sharks are frequently spotted at Maracaibo, but you can't count on them. Blacktips (several closely related species) are most common, but it is possible to encounter hammerheads, shortfin makos, lemons, tigers, bulls or others. Keep in mind, though, that you pay your money and you take your chances. Some years few sharks are seen, and other years sharks are seen on most dives. Big schools of eagle rays and mantas have also been seen at Maracaibo.

STEVE ROSENBERG

17 Colombia Shallows

Colombia Shallows is inshore of Colombia Reef. A convenient two-tank day of diving would start on the wall at Colombia and move in to the Shallows for a second dive. However, Colombia Shallows is less often visited because most boat operators from town prefer to take divers to Paraíso, Yocab, or other more northerly reefs (near lunch and home port) on their second dive of the day. Boats that stop at San Francisco Beach between dives almost certainly will not turn around and run south to Colombia Shallows after lunch, so if you want to dive these southerly

Typical Depth Range:
    20-40 feet (6-12 meters)
Typical Current Conditions: Light
Access: Boat
Expertise Required: Novice

reefs back-to-back, be sure to make the necessary arrangements before leaving the dock.

Colombia Shallows is a good area for beginners, since currents tend to be light

L. MARTIN

Colombia Shallows is made of huge vertical coral formations that rise toward the surface from a sand bottom at about 40 feet.

and there's lots of clear space to sit down on sand and between walls of coral. It's a great place to practice hovering. It's like a miniature Palancar Reef without hordes of other divers. Furthermore, the restricted bottom depth lets photographers take wall-type shots without fear of dropping off into an abyss while focusing. Snorkeling is excellent above the coral heads, but look out for boat traffic!

18 Sand Diver's Secret

If you enjoy diving away from the crowds, and need a change of scene, Sand Diver's Secret is for you. You won't find it on the map, but you already know how to get there – just stop on the way to or from your favorite reef, or take a detour away from the dropoff out onto the sand. Chances are good that your fellow divers will think you've lost your way. You can surprise them when you bring back a detailed log and a roll of film of all the things you saw on the sand that they didn't see. Most of the diving on Cozumel takes place over reefs, which account for a very small fraction of the actual diveable area. There is a lot more sand than coral. Divers who get dropped

Typical Depth Range: Wherever you find sand flats

Typical Current Conditions: The full spectrum, from none to strong

Access: Boat or shore

Expertise Required: Novice

over sand flats usually keep their heads up and their fins moving until they find "the dive site" (i.e., the coral). They thereby miss some of the most interesting animals and one of the most fascinating habitats underwater. That's the Sand Diver's Secret.

The conch's eye is at the end of a stalk.

L. MARTIN

A diver discovers a heart urchin in the sand flats.

L. MARTIN

A closeup inspection of the sand flats can reveal creatures not found on the reefs.

To appreciate the sand flats properly, you'll have to get right down on the deck with your mask a few inches from the sand. Notice that the sediment differs in coarseness from one sand flat to another, and within a sand flat from spot to spot. The smallest particles collect where current velocities are lowest, and vice versa. Water movement can easily carry off fine particles, whereas coarse, gravely sand requires faster currents to move it. The texture of the sand provides an index of the average current velocity. Big chunks indicate high speeds. Fine, soft sand means low current velocity.

The patterns of marks in the sand can also tell you something about water move-ment and direction. High-speed currents heap coarse particles into big sand waves, while slower currents produce only ripple marks in finer sand. Larger sand particles are found toward the tops of the sand waves or ripples, and finer particles collect in the quieter water in the troughs between the waves. Ripples and sand waves are oriented 90° to the average direction of water movement, just like sea fans, and can therefore be used to help you navigate on the bottom.

Many so-called "infaunal" animals live in sandy environments, including clams, burrowing shrimps and other crustaceans, and worms. Most of them are large enough to see, but remain buried below

You will have to be very alert to spot animals such as this crab, which is colored like the sand and is often buried with only its back and eye stalks visible.

the surface where they are invisible to divers. Deeper burrowers have tubes leading to the surface so that they can get food and oxygen, and discharge wastes. Infauna sometimes filter plankton from the water, or feed on microscopic "meiofauna," tiny animals that live between the sand grains, forever wandering in a maze of particles that must seem as huge as boulders to them.

"Epibenthic" animals live on or near the surface of the sand, sometimes feeding on infauna or other small attached plants. Some epibenthic animals are tiny, such as the schools of clear mysid crustaceans (the size of brine shrimp) that usually are mistaken for juvenile fishes. Larger forms include heart urchins, hermit crabs, and conchs, which can be found by following their tracks across the sand. Heart urchin tracks look like meandering ridges a couple of inches high. Conchs leave a smooth groove. Hermit crab tracks show small depressions where their legs touch the bottom and an irregular trough where the shell drags. Sea stars, long-spined urchins, and big snails such as tritons are also promi-

nent epibenthic beasts. Because other animals eat them too, quite a few epibenthic species are nocturnal, spending the daytime buried in the sand or beneath the edges of coral heads.

A variety of predatory fishes feed on infaunal and epibenthic animals. Rays, peacock flounders, guitarfishes, and skates treat the sand flats as a cafeteria with an excellent selection, open 24 hours a day. Stingrays dig obvious pits in the sand by flapping their "wings" and excavating worms and clams. These pits are sometimes six feet across and several feet deep. Other fishes such as bar jacks and smooth trunkfishes hover above feeding rays, picking out any stray infaunal animals that are stirred up by the rays. If rays aren't working, trunkfishes can do their own smaller excavations by blowing water out of their mouths onto the sand. You can attract both bar jacks and trunkfishes by simulating a ray, and digging a pit. Many fishes will be attracted to the sand plume you create, hoping to find themselves a snack.

We hope you won't simply pass over the sand flats on your way to the coral. As long as you're burning air and time, why not have a good look around?

The peacock flounder can change colors to blend in with the bottom.

Marine Life

Cozumel has the usual suite of Caribbean reef fish, invertebrates, and plants. Some of the species likely to be seen are described in this section. Divers will notice a definite zonation of groups of species that changes with increasing depth

and distance from shore. The zonation reflects decreasing levels of light and wave exposure with increasing depth, and increasing current velocities off-shore. The zonation is most obvious among such reef-forming invertebrates as corals and sponges, but many fish are closely associated with the reef-builders and so show zonation themselves.

A diver and gray angelfish on Yocab Reef.

Corals

Very close to shore, perhaps the most prominent species is the elkhorn coral. It forms huge colonies that shelter long-spined sea urchins during the daytime. At night, the urchins move away from their shelters and graze on plants on the surrounding bottom. The largest gorgonians, or sea fans and sea whips, are near shore too. Divers are more likely to encounter fire coral in shallow water, growing on gorgonian skeletons, dead coral, or other surfaces.

Farther from shore, most of the reefs are dominated by the mountainous star coral and the cavernous star coral. In shallow water, these tend to grow as large mounds. As you probably know, corals are animals, but they have internal plants (zooxanthellae), which produce food and oxygen that are used by their hosts. The zooxanthellae need light to exist, and many species of corals change their growth forms depending on where they

Fungus coral grows best at the base of coral heads.

live in order to capture as much light as possible for their zooxanthellae. As a result, in deeper water (where there is not as much light), species such as the star corals tend to form sheets or plates that act like natural solar collectors. The large buttresses, such as those on Palancar Reef, are built mainly by star corals, and the various growth forms can be seen at different depths. Species can always be recognized by the shape of the individual polyps, whatever the shape of the entire colony. The massive corals, such as the giant brain coral, are found over a wide depth range but are often larger in deeper water.

Other corals, such as the sheet or plate corals, specialize in living in low-light situations (crevices, overhangs, or deep water). These corals can become very large, thin, and fragile at depths where they are not likely to be broken by waves.

G. LEWBEL

Fire corals come in a variety of shapes and sizes, but are usually characterized by white tips at the end.

Anemones & Sponges

The giant anemone is frequently seen with fluorescent tentacle tips, which bear the stinging cells it uses to capture tiny crustaceans and other prey. Different colored tentacles do not indicate different species but rather color phases of the same species.

Sponges

There are sponges wherever coral is found in Cozumel, and large sponges can be seen on nearly every dive. Look for brittle stars in purple vase sponges. Bristle worms (also called fire worms) are common everywhere, but can be seen breeding on purple vase sponges at night during the late fall. Many sponges look brown by daylight but are orange or blood-red by night or in strobe-lit photographs. The basket sponges on the dropoffs have grown into funnel shapes under the influence of the usual south-to-north current. Their open cavities face north so that more stagnant water (carrying wastes from the sponge) is extracted from the funnel by passing current, and water with food and oxygen surrounds the outer filtering surface of the sponge.

Giant anemones are common on the reefs surrounding Cozumel.

Fishes

Fishes on Cozumel are extremely diverse, and most of the abundant reef species in the Caribbean can be seen at one time or another by divers on Cozumel. A few common nearshore species include yellow stingrays, barracudas, black groupers (handfed and tamed by divers on Palancar and Santa Rosa reefs), moray eels, angelfishes, butterfly-fishes, wrasses, barjacks, grunts, snappers, and triggerfish. Chubs and yellow and black barred sergeant-majors will surround you, begging for food. Damselfishes will nip at you on every reef, and various par-rotfishes can be seen and heard breaking coral with their jaws. Big-eye, glasseye snappers, and glassy sweepers are often seen hiding in shaded crevices in the daytime. Despite the temptation to feed fish, keep in mind the practice is generally frowned upon, as it upsets normal fish eating habits and can encour-age aggressive behavior.

Most photographers will want to search under coral heads at the edge of sandy patches for the elusive, splendid toadfish, a magnificent species in a family of fishes otherwise not known for their beauty. The splendid toadfish is believed to be common only in the vicinity of Cozumel. While looking under ledges for toadfish, you may also see large spiny lobsters and crabs.

Whitespotted filefish

Parrotfish

Porkfish

Masked hamlet

Common Hazardous Marine Animals

Sea Urchins The most common hazardous animal divers will encounter around Cozumel is the long-spined sea urchin. This urchin has spines capable of penetrating wetsuits, booties, and gloves like a knife through butter. Injuries are nearly always immediately painful, and sometimes infect. Urchins are found at every diving depth, although they are more common in shallow water near shore, especially under coral heads. At night the urchins come out of their hiding places and are even easier to bump into. Minor injuries can be

Long-spined sea urchin

dealt with by extracting the spines (easier said than done!) and treating the wound with antibiotic cream. Make sure your tetanus immunization is current; serious punctures will require a doctor's attention.

Fire Coral Fire coral is most common in shallow water, but can grow as an encrusting form on dead gorgonians or coral at any depth. A creamy tan or mustard in color, with white tips at the end, it comes in a variety of shapes. Because it can overgrow other coral, such as sea fans, it is not always easy to distinguish. Upon contact the nematocysts, small stinging cells located on the polyps, will discharge, causing a burning sensation that usually goes away in a minute or two. In some individuals, contact results in red welts. Cortisone cream can reduce the inflammation. Coral cuts and scrapes

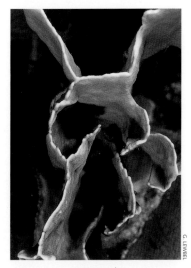
Fire coral

can also irritate and frequently infect. We've treated minor coral scratches successfully with antibiotic cream, but serious cuts should be handled by a doctor, especially if broken bits of coral are embedded in the wound.

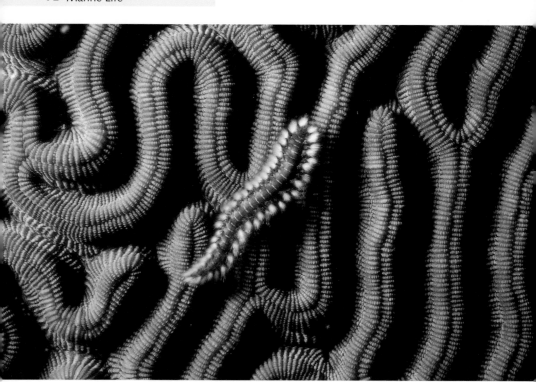

G. LEWBEL

A bristle worm makes its way across a giant brain coral colony.

Bristle or Fire Worms Bristle worms, also called fire worms, can be found on most reefs with a little searching. If you touch one with bare skin it will embed tiny, stinging bristles in your skin and cause a burning sensation that may be followed by the development of a red spot or welt. The sensation is similar to touching fire coral or massaging one of those fuzzy, soft-looking cactuses on land. The bristles will eventually work their way out of your skin in a couple of days. You can try to scrape them off with the edge of a sharp knife. Cortisone cream helps reduce local inflammation.

Sponges Sponges also have fine spicules, and some species (so-called fire sponges) have a chemical irritant that is immediately painful. Although bright red color is sometimes a clue to the bad ones, it's not completely reliable. We have been stung by various innocuous-looking

G. LEWBEL

sponges. If you get spicules in your skin, try scraping them off with the edge of a sharp knife. We've also tried pouring mild vinegar solutions and mild ammonia solutions on the parts that hurt; sometimes they work, sometimes they don't. The stinging sensation usually goes away within a day, and cortisone cream helps.

Moray Eels Moray eels are dangerous only if approached too closely or harassed. There are lots of morays under coral heads and in crevices. In recent years, divers at other islands have hand-fed morays, but this practice has not yet become widespread on  Cozumel. Green morays seem to be especially feisty. One of the authors who was involved in a scientific fish-tagging experiment can attest personally to the biting ability of green morays (number of needle-like teeth, penetration depth, number of stitches required, etc.). Bites are sometimes infective and very painful and call for a doctor's attention.

Moray eels are frequently seen in coral heads and crevices during the day. They normally leave their protected recesses at night to hunt.

Rays Sand flats around Cozumel are inhabited by two species of stingrays, the southern stingray (very large, wary, and difficult to approach), and the yellow stingray (small, well-camouflaged, and easy to approach). Stingrays are not especially aggressive, but they don't take kindly to being sat on, patted, or stepped on. If you leave them alone, they'll leave you alone. If you insist on a 1:1 macro shot of a stingray nostril you will probably be stung by the long, barbed stinger at the base of the tail. Wounds are always extremely painful, and often deep and infective, and can cause serious symptoms including anaphylactic shock. If you get stung, head for the hospital.

Scorpionfish Scorpionfish are well-camouflaged, small fish (usually less than a foot long) that have poisonous spines hidden among their fins. They are often difficult to spot, since they typically sit quietly on the bottom looking more like plant-covered rocks than fish. As with stingrays, watch where you put your hands and knees and you're not likely to meet one the hard way. If you get stung, severe allergic reactions are quite possible and great pain and infection are virtually certain, so head for the hospital and see a doctor.

A well-camouflaged spotted scorpionfish rests almost motionless on a rocky surface.

STEVE ROSENBERG

Caribbean reef shark

Sharks Sharks are very uncommon at most of the reefs around Cozumel. Sharks are reported more often at Maracaibo Reef than other sites, and nurse sharks are sometimes spotted sleeping under ledges at Yocab and San Juan reefs. Please don't tug on nurse sharks' tails while they are asleep, by the way, even though it's tempting. They wake up grumpy and have bitten a number of divers in other locations. Any shark injury obviously calls for immediate medical attention.

G. LEWBEL

Barracudas are often difficult for divers to approach. The best tactic for getting a closer look is to hold still and wait for them to investigate you.

Barracuda Barracudas are included in this section mainly because of their undeserved reputation for ferocity. There are a few reports of attacks on swimmers in dirty water in other locations, but on Cozumel, you'll be lucky to get one close enough for a good photograph. At night, though, you can sometimes get very near to a sleeping barracuda.

Diving Safety

L. MARTIN

This section discusses common hazards, including emergency procedures in case of a diving accident. We do not discuss the diagnosis or treatment of serious medical problems; refer to your first aid manual or emergency diving accident manual for that information.

We do suggest some ways to contact qualified medical personnel as rapidly as possible, based partly on responses to our own inquiries for this volume and partly on information supplied by other sources. Emergency contact information can change unpredictably when personnel and facilities move, get new telephone numbers, and so on. Be sure to check on emergency contact information during or just prior to your dive trip.

Diving Accidents

In case of a diving accident, such as a lung overpressure injury (e.g. air embolism, pneumothorax, mediastinal emphysema) or decompression sickness ("bends"), prompt recompression treatment in a chamber may be essential to prevent permanent injury or death.

Hyperbaric Chambers There are currently two functional recompresssion chambers on Cozumel Island: the hospital and the Buceo Medico Mexicano (B.M.M.) chambers. The older facility is at the hospital (Centro de Salud), a few blocks from the water on Calle 11 Sur., which intersects Avenida Rafael Melgar (the street along the waterfront) near the Hotel Barracuda, toward the southern side of town (☎ 2-01-40).

The hospital will recompress you if the other chamber is occupied, or if you prefer to go the low-budget route. Because the hospital is government funded, the cost of a chamber treatment may be as low as several hundred U.S. dollars. However, the hospital chamber is used mainly for non-diving-related hyperbaric oxygen treatments and for injured Mexican nationals,

Diving and Flying

Most divers to Cozumel get there by plane. While it's fine to dive soon *after* flying, it's important to remember that your last dive should be completed at least 12 hours (some experts advise 24 hours) *before* your flight to minimize the risk of residual nitrogen in the blood that can cause decompression injury.

rather than for tourists. If you look as if you can afford the high-priced spread, you will probably find yourself shunted to the B.M.M. chamber. This may be to your advantage. In the past, reports on the hospital's chamber have been mixed, and, frankly, recompression therapy seems like a bad place to save money.

The B.M.M. chamber, a member of the international Subaquatic Safety Services Recompression Facilities Network (S.S.S.), is geared specifically for diving tourists. It is located on Calle 5 Sur, around the corner from Aqua Safari and about one block from the water (☎ 2-14-30).

Dive operators can choose to be affiliated with the chamber. Affiliates, who tend to be better established, charge their clients US$1 per day for this affiliation, and pass this money on to the chamber. The money ensures that the staff and supplies will be on hand day and night, and helps to reduce the chamber's dependency on use fees. While diving with an operator who has agreed to this arrangement, you are guaranteed access to the chamber and its attending medical staff without cost if you are injured on a dive, even if you have no medical insurance to cover the charges. If you do have insurance, S.S.S. will bill your insurance company after you have been treated. However, none of these costs will be passed onto you, even if your insurance company drags its feet or doesn't pay at all. To add a personal note, the authors will not dive with any Cozumel operator who is not affiliated with the B.M.M. chamber.

If you need an ambulance, call the Red Cross (☎ 2-10-58). B.M.M. can also set up ambulance transportation and simultaneously prepare for your arrival at the chamber, and can assist you in locating other physicians for non-diving problems.

It should be emphasized that the chamber situation may be completely different by the time you arrive on Cozumel. Emergency numbers change, and chambers wax and wane depending upon their funding and staff. We strongly recommend that you ask your booking agent to provide you with reliable emergency information at the time you make your reservations. Furthermore, we suggest that you check this information with DAN (see below), given the state of flux in Mexico. Upon arrival, we also suggest you ask your dive operator how to cope with a diving emergency or other accident. Don't accept a vague answer. You should interpret the absence of a workable accident management plan as a lack of both professionalism and concern for your welfare.

If this all sounds a little paranoid, be warned that it isn't. Some of those old horror stories about botched evacuations and bungled recompression treatments in Cozumel are true. It's a long way back to the U.S. if you have a medical problem. The trip may involve extensive bureaucratic juggling, expense, and delays. Keep an eye on your gauges, make slow ascents and safety stops, and here – more than many other places – don't push your luck.

DAN Divers Alert Network (DAN) is an international membership association of individuals and organizations sharing a common interest in diving and safety. It operates a 24-hour diving emergency hotline, ☎ 919-684-8111 or ☎ 919-684-4DAN (☎ 919-684-4DAN accepts collect calls in a dive emergency). DAN does not directly provide medical care; however, it does provide advice on early treatment, evacuation, and hyperbaric treatment of diving-related injuries. Divers should contact DAN for assistance as soon as a diving emergency is suspected. DAN membership is reasonably priced and includes DAN TravelAssist, a membership benefit, which covers medical air evacuation from anywhere in the world for any illness or injury. For a small additional fee, divers can get secondary insurance coverage for decompression illness. For membership questions, ☎ 800-446-2671 in the U.S. or ☎ 919-684-2948 elsewhere.

Air Ambulance Service If you elect to leave Cozumel for treatment, you are probably going to need a chartered flight with medical equipment and personnel on board, in an aircraft capable of pressurization at the equivalent of sea-level (1 atmosphere). Several air ambulance companies in the United States can provide this service, but flying in Mexico requires some red tape that is best taken care of in advance. Under ideal circumstances you will probably wait at least four hours after you request an aircraft before it lands in Cozumel.

Emergency Contacts

Recompression Chambers (Cozumel):
Hospital: ☎ 2-01-40
B.M.M.: ☎ 2-14-30
Divers Alert Network (DAN):
☎ 919-684-8111 or ☎ 919-684-4326 (for assistance in dealing with Cozumel recompression chambers or for finding a chamber in the U.S., or to arrange evacuation for a diving emergency)

L. MARTIN

Boat traffic is a serious hazard in Cozumel. Be especially alert for boat noise,
look around during ascents when near the surface, and be proficient at
buoyancy control during ascents and while performing safety stops.

You should be aware that the cost of an evacuation flight will be
high and that payment will be expected either in Mexico or promptly
after arrival in the U.S. You will most likely be asked to provide proof
of financial responsibility in the form of cash, check, or credit cards,
or to furnish names and phone numbers of friends or relatives in the
States who will guarantee the cost of the flight. Brace yourself for a
bill that may exceed the price of a new car, depending on how fast an
aircraft you need (this may be your chance to ride in a Lear jet),
what medical equipment and personnel need to be on board, its
point of origin, and its destination. Alternatively, if you are a
DAN member, you also have DAN's evacuation service. DAN's TravelAssist program provides its members with air ambulance coverage
for diving and non-diving emergencies. PADI also provides similar
kinds of insurance.

Diving Conservation & Awareness

L. MARTIN

Dive sites tend to be located where the reefs and walls display the most beautiful corals and sponges. It only takes a moment – an inadvertently placed hand or knee on the coral or an unaware brush or kick with a fin – to destroy this fragile living part of our delicate ecosystem. Please consider the following tips when diving and help preserve the ecology and beauty of the reefs:

1. Maintain proper buoyancy control and avoid over-weighting. Be aware that buoyancy can change over the period of an extended trip: initially you may breathe harder and need more weighting; a few days later you may breath more easily and need less weight.

2. Use correct weight belt position to stay horizontal, i.e., raise the belt above your waist to elevate your feet/fins, and move it lower toward your hips to lower them.

3. Use your tank position in the backpack as a balance weight, i.e., raise your backpack on the tank to lower your legs, and lower the backpack on the tank to raise your legs.

4. Be careful about buoyancy loss at depth; the deeper you go the more your wetsuit compresses, and the more buoyancy you lose.

5. Photographers must be extra careful. Cameras and equipment affect buoyancy. Changing f-stops, framing a subject, and maintaining position for a photo often conspire to prohibit the ideal "no-touch" approach on a reef. So, when you must use "hold-fasts," choose them intelligently (i.e., use one finger only for leverage off an area of dead coral).

6. Avoid full leg kicks when working close to the bottom and when leaving a photo scene. When you inadvertently kick something, stop kicking! Seems obvious, but some divers either semi-panic or are totally oblivious when they bump something. When treading water in shallow reef areas, take care not to kick up clouds of sand. Settling sand can easily smother the delicate organisms of the reef.

L. MARTIN

Controlling your buoyancy is one of the most important skills you can learn to help prevent inadvertent damage to the reef.

L. MARTIN

Reputable dive operators on Cozumel strongly advocate a "no touch" policy
for divers exploring the reefs.

7. When swimming in strong currents, be extra careful about leg kicks and hand-holds.

8. Attach dangling gauges, computer consoles, and octopus regulators. They are like miniature wrecking balls to a reef.

9. Never drop boat anchors onto a coral reef, and take care not to ground boats on coral. Encourage dive operators and regulatory bodies to establish permanent moorings at popular dive sites.

10. Resist the temptation to collect or buy corals or shells. Aside from the ecological damage, taking home marine souvenirs depletes the beauty of a site and spoils the enjoyment of others.

11. Resist the temptation to feed fish. You may disturb their normal eating habits, encourage aggressive behavior, or feed them food that is detrimental to their health.

Marine Conservation Organizations

Coral reefs and oceans are facing unprecedented environmental pressures. The following groups are actively involved in promoting responsible diving practices, publicizing environmental marine threats, and lobbying for better policies.

Project AWARE Foundation
☎ 714-540-0251
Website: www.projectaware.org

Cousteau Society
☎ 757-523-9335
Website: www.cousteau.org

CORAL: The Coral Reef Alliance
☎ 510-848-0110
Website: www.coral.org/

Ocean Futures
☎ 714-456-0790
Website: www.oceanfutures.org

Coral Forest
☎ 415-788-REEF
Website: www.blacktop.com/
coralforest/

ReefKeeper International
☎ 305-358-4600
Website: www.reefkeeper.org

L. MARTIN

When diving in Cozumel's waters, you are diving in a national preserve. The Mexican government considers illegal collecting and spearfishing a serious offense.

Spearfishing & Hunting Underwater

Virtually all of the island's diveable reefs lie within a Mexican national preserve, Parque Marino Nacional Arrecifes de Cozumel. The park extends from Paraíso Reef all the way around the southern end of Cozumel. Collection of any animals (including shells with living inhabitants) or plants within the preserve is strictly forbidden as is damaging any part of the reefs. Outside of the preserve, sport fishing is allowed if you have a Mexican fishing license.

The Mexican game fishing regulations are fairly complex, and include bag and seasonal restrictions on many species. Fishing licenses can be requested from the Oficina de Pesca (Fish Office) in San Miguel on Cozumel (ask a taxi driver where it is), or from the charter sport fishing boat captains who can obtain licenses for their clients. Prices for the licenses currently are changing but have been nominal in the past for short trips. Take the time to ask for a copy of the most recent regulations, though, and ask specifically about diving requirements. Be careful! The Mexican government takes illegal collecting very seriously, and a large fine including confiscation of the gear used for the collection (i.e., all of your diving equipment and the boat) would not be out of the ordinary. Spear guns are usually seized by customs upon entry to Cozumel, just in case you might be tempted to stray, and returned to you (perhaps) when you leave.

Dive Services

L. MARTIN

The following dive operators are affiliated with the privately owned Buceo Medico Mexicano (B.M.M.) recompression chamber in San Miguel. The list of affiliates changes rapidly. To verify affiliation before you book dives with an operator, call the chamber at ☎ 2-23-87. The email address is: servicios@cozunet.finred.com.mx, and the website is: www.islacozumel.net/services/buceomed/#SSS

To call Cozumel, dial your international access code for the country you are calling from (in the U.S. it's **011**), **+52+987** before dialing the 5-digit local number.

Albatross Charters ☎ 2-56-19	**Buena Ventura** ☎ 2-17-74	**DIMI** ☎ 2-29-15
Aldora Divers ☎ 2-40-48	**Caballito del Cbe.** ☎ 2-14-49	**Discover Dive Shop** ☎ 2-02-80
Aqua Safari ☎ 2-01-01	**Caribbean Divers** ☎ 2-10-80	**Dive Cozumel** ☎ 2-41-10
Aqua World ☎ 2-07-00	**Carlo Scuba** ☎ 2-01-99	**Dive House** ☎ 2-19-53
B & B Divers ☎ 4-74-01	**Cha Cha Cha** ☎ 2-23-31	**Dive Memo** ☎ 2-20 67
Black Shark Dive Shop ☎ 2-03-96	**Cozumel Equalizers** ☎ 2-35-11	**Dive Paradise** ☎ 2-10-07
Blue Angel ☎ 2-16-31	**Deep Blue** ☎ 2-56-53	**Dive with Martin** ☎ 2-26-10
Blue Bubble Divers ☎ 2-18-65	**Del Mar Aquatics** ☎ 2-18-33	**Diving Adventures** ☎ 2-30-09
Blue Note ☎ 2-03-12	**Diamante** ☎ 2-34-43	**Eco Divers** ☎ 2-56-28

El Pulpo
☎ 2-00-50

Flash Adventures
☎ 2-05-70

Island Divers
☎ 2-36-79

La Tortuga
☎ 2-53-81

Let's Go
☎ 2-55-66

Manta Raya Divers
☎ 2-06-84

Marine Sports
☎ 2-29-22

Mexico Diving Explorer
☎ 2-08-80

Palancar Fish Eye
☎ 2-27-53

Pascual Scuba
☎ 2-54-54

Playa Corona
☎ 2-15-02

Quetzal Divers
☎ 2-44-52

Sand Dollar Sport
☎ 2-55-66

Robertaís Scuba
☎ 2-44-87

Scuba
☎ 2-16-63

Scuba Cuzamil
☎ 2-06-27

Scuba Du
☎ 2-19-94

Scuba Shack
☎ 2-42-40

Sea Scuba
☎ 2-37-78

Sea Urchin Dive
☎ 2-45-17

Seafari Divers
☎ 2-56-50

Snorkel Center
☎ 2-04-77

Staff Divers
☎ 2-07-55

Studio Blue
☎ 2-43-30

Wildcat Divers
☎ 2-10-28

Yucatech Expeditions
☎ 2-46-18

Index

dive sites covered in this book appear in **bold** type

A

accidents, diving 76
accommodations *see* hotels
advanced diver 31
air ambulance service 78-79
Airplane Flats *see* **Junkyard, The**
anemones 35, 53, 58, 69
angelfish 38, 39, 49, 53, 66, 70

B

B.M.M. (Buceo Medico Mexicano)
    see recompression chamber
barracuda 45, 70, 75
Beachcomber Cavern 41-43
Bermuda chub 38
blue chromis 34
boat traffic 27
bristle worms 69, 72

C

Cancún 18
car rental 19
Cardona Reef 51-52
cave dives 41-42
cenote 14
certification card 22
chamber *see* recompression chamber
Chankanab 40
Christ of the Abyss 40
citizenship, proof of 22
collecting, underwater 82, 84
Colombia Reef 58
Colombia Shallows 60-61
conch 53, 62
conservation 80-82
    - organizations 83
coral 67
    - cavernous sea 29, 67
    - elkhorn 37
    - fire 67, 68, 71
    - fungus 67
    - giant brain 68
    - plate 58, 68
currency *see* money
currents 23

D

damselfish 37, 70
    - sergeant major 38, 70
DAN (Divers Alert Network) 78
decompression sickness 76
departure tax 22
Devil's Throat 56
dining 20
dive boats 25-26
dive operators 23-25
dive services 85-86
diving recommendations 30
diving techniques 27-28
documents 22
dress, style 20
drift diving 27-28
driver's license 22

E

eel *see* moray
El Paso del Cedral Reef 48
embolism 76
emergency contacts 78
epibenthic animals 65

F

ferries 18
filefish 38, 45, 47, 70
fire coral *see* coral
fire worms *see* bristle worms
fishes, identification 70
fishing licenses 84

flying to Cozumel 18
flying and diving 77

G

gorgonians 36, 40, 58, 67
Green Mirror, The 42
grouper 45, 49, 55, 70
grunt 12, 40
   - bluestriped 12, 48
   - French 12, 38, 48

H

hamlet, masked 70
hazards *see* safety
hazardous marine life 71
history 11
Horseshoe, the 55
hospital 76-77
hotels 16
hunting, underwater 84
hyperbaric chamber
     see recompression chamber

I

infaunal animals 64-65
intermediate diver 31
International Pier 18. 36
ironshore 14, 28, 42

J

Junkyard, The 36-38

L

language 19
la Turista 20
"live boat" 27
lobster 44, 47, 70

M

Maracaibo Reef 59-60
marine life 66
marine conservation *see* conservation

Mayan culture 11-12
Mayan ruins 11
meiofauna 65
money 19
Montezuma's revenge 20

N

national preserve 83, 84
night diving 36
natural history 14
nocturnal fishes 43, 52, 53
novice diver 31

O

octopus 38

P

Palancar Gardens 55
Palancar Reef 55
Paradise *see* Paraíso
Paraíso Reef North 34-35
Paraíso Reef South 38-39
parrotfish 37, 49, 51, 70
passport 22
porkfish 48, 70
Punta Sur 56-57

Q

Quintana Roo 11

R

rating system 31
ray, eagle 49
recompression chamber 25, 76-77

S

safety 76
San Francisco Beach 26, 49, 51, 60
San Francisco Reef 53
San Gervasio ruins 11
San Miguel de Cozumel 15
Sand Diver's Secret 62-65

Santa Rosa Reef 54-55
scorpionfish 74
sea cucumber 39
sea urchins 37, 51, 71
sharks 60, 75
  - nurse 44
shopping 20
shore diving 27
signal device 27
silver fingerling 41
snapper 40, 48, 70
snorkel (snorkeler)
   36, 38, 40, 60, 62
souvenirs 20-21
spearfishing 84
sponge rash 50
sponges 50, 69, 72-73
stingrays 53, 65, 70, 74
sweeper 43, 70

T

taxis 19, 28
thermocline 42
tipping 17

toadfish 35, 70
Tormentos Reef 44-45
tourist permit 22
transportation 18
travel documents 22
triggerfish 70
trunkfish 46, 65
Tunich Reef 49-50

W

wall diving
   30, 53, 54, 55, 56, 58, 59
water, purified 20
weather 14
wrasse 70

Y

Yocab Reef 46-47

Z

zonation 66
zooxanthellae 67-68

Notes

Lonely Planet Pisces Books

The **Diving & Snorkeling Guides** are dive guides to top destinations worldwide. Beautifully illustrated with full-color photos throughout, the series explores the best diving and snorkeling areas and prepares divers for what to expect when they get there. Each site is described in detail, with information on suggested ability levels, depth, visibility, and, of course, marine life. There's basic topside information as well for each destination. Don't miss the guides to:

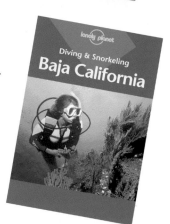

Australia: Coral Sea & Great Barrier Reef

Australia: Southeast Coast

Bahamas: Family Islands & Grand

Bahamas: Nassau & New Providence

Bali & the Komodo Region

Belize

Bermuda

Best Caribbean Diving

Bonaire

British Virgin Islands

Cayman Islands

Cocos Island

Cozumel

Cuba

Curaçao

Fiji

Florida Keys

Florida's East Coast

Guam & Yap

Hawaiian Islands

Jamaica

Northern California & Monterey Peninsula

Pacific Northwest

Palau

Puerto Rico

Red Sea

Roatan & Honduras' Bay Islands

Scotland

Seychelles

Southern California

St. Maarten, Saba, & St. Eustatius

Texas

Truk Lagoon

Turks & Caicos

U.S. Virgin Islands

Vanuatu

Plus illustrated natural history guides:

Pisces Guide to Caribbean Reef Ecology

Great Reefs of the World

Sharks of Tropical & Temperate Seas

Venomous & Toxic Marine Life of the World

Watching Fishes

Lonely Planet Series Descriptions

Lonely Planet **travel guides** explore a destination in depth with options to suit a range of budgets. With reliable, practical advice on getting around, restaurants and accommodations, these easy-to-use guides also include detailed maps, color photographs, extensive background material and coverage of sites both on and off the beaten track.

For budget travelers **shoestring guides** are the best single source of travel information covering an entire continent or large region. Written by experienced travelers these 'tried and true' classics offer reliable, first-hand advice on transportation, restaurants and accommodations, and insider tips for avoiding bureaucratic confusion and stretching money as far as possible.

City guides cover many of the world's great cities with full-color photographs throughout, front and back cover gatefold maps, and information for every traveler's budget and style. With information for business travelers, all the best places to eat and shop and itinerary suggestions for long and short-term visitors, city guides are a complete package.

Lonely Planet **phrasebooks** have essential words and phrases to help travelers communicate with the locals. With color tabs for quick reference, an extensive vocabulary, use of local scripts and easy-to-follow pronunciation instructions, these handy, pocket-sized language guides cover most situations a traveler is likely to encounter.

Lonely Planet **walking guides** cover some of the world's most exciting trails. With detailed route descriptions including degrees of difficulty and best times to go, reliable maps and extensive background information, these guides are an invaluable resource for both independent hikers and those in organized groups.

Lonely Planet **travel atlases** are thoroughly researched and fact-checked by the guidebook authors to ensure they complement the books. And the handy format means none of the holes, wrinkles, tears, or constant folding and refolding of flat maps. They include background information in five languages.

Journeys is a new series of travel literature that captures the spirit of a place, illuminates a culture, recounts an adventure and introduces a fascinating way of life. Written by a diverse group of writers, they are tales to read while on the road or at home in your favorite armchair.

Entertaining, independent and adventurous, Lonely Planet **videos** encourage the same approach to travel as the guidebooks. Currently broadcast throughout the world, this award-winning series features all original footage and music.

Planet Talk

Lonely Planet's FREE quarterly newsletter

We love hearing from our readers and think you'd like to hear from us.

When... is the best time to see nurse sharks in Belize?

Where... can you hear the best palm-wine music in Ghana?

How... do you get from Asunción to Areguá by steam train?

What... is the best way to see India?

For the answer to these and many other questions read PLANET TALK.

Every issue is packed with up-to-date travel news and advice including:

- a letter from Lonely Planet founders Tony and Maureen Wheeler
- travel diary from a Lonely Planet author–find out what it's really like out on the road
- feature article on an important and topical travel issue
- a selection of recent letters from our readers
- the latest travel news from all over the world
- details on Lonely Planet's new and forthcoming releases

To join our mailing list contact any Lonely Planet office.

Lonely Planet Online

Get the latest travel information before you leave or while you're on the road

Whether you've just begun planning your next trip, or you're chasing down specific info on currency regulations or visa requirements, check out Lonely Planet Online for up-to-the-minute travel information.

As well as travel profiles of your favorite destinations (including maps and photos), you'll find current reports from our researchers and other travelers, updates on health and visas, travel advisories, and discussion of the ecological and political issues you need to be aware of as you travel.

There's also an online travelers' forum where you can share your experience of life on the road, meet travel companions and ask other travelers for their recommendations and advice. We also have plenty of links to other online sites useful to independent travelers.

And of course we have a complete and up-to-date list of all Lonely Planet travel products including guides, phrasebooks, atlases, Journeys and videos and a simple online ordering facility if you can't find the book you want elsewhere.

www.lonelyplanet.com or AOL keyword: lp

Travel news goes off faster than a bag of prawns in the sun.

Comet

Lonely Planet's new monthly email newsletter, **Comet**, brings you the latest travel news, destination ideas, travel tips, health advice, travellers' yarns, raging debates and competitions. All this, and it's free.

To subscribe just enter your email at:
http://www.lonelyplanet.com/comet/

Where to Find Us . . .

Lonely Planet is known worldwide for publishing practical, reliable and no-nonsense travel information in our guides and on our web site. The Lonely Planet list covers just about every accessible part of the world. Currently there are nine series: *Pisces guides, travel guides, shoestring guides, walking guides, city guides, phrasebooks, audio packs, travel atlases* and *Journeys*–a unique collection of travel writing.

Lonely Planet Publications

Australia
PO Box 617, Hawthorn 3122, Victoria
☎ (03) 9819 1877 fax (03) 9819 6459
e-mail talk2us@lonelyplanet.com.au

USA
150 Linden Street
Oakland, California 94607
☎ (510) 893 8555, (800) 275 8555
fax (510) 893 8563
e-mail info@lonelyplanet.com

UK
10A Spring Place,
London NW5 3BH
☎ (0171) 428 4800 fax (0171) 428 4828
e-mail go@lonelyplanet.co.uk

France
71 bis rue du Cardinal Lemoine,
75005 Paris
☎ 01 44 32 06 20 fax 01 46 34 72 55
e-mail bip@lonelyplanet.fr

World Wide Web: www.lonelyplanet.com or **AOL keyword: lp**